Dogs
&Autism

Annie Bowes, DVM

Dogs & Autism
All marketing and publishing rights guaranteed to and reserved by:

FUTURE HORIZONS INC.

721 W. Abram Street
Arlington, TX 76013
(800) 489-0727
(817) 277-0727
(817) 277-2270 (fax)
E-mail: info@fhautism.com
www.fhautism.com

Cover & interior design by John Yacio III

ISBN: 9781941765906

To my husband, for always being my hero and supporting my passion for dogs.

Contents

Dogs & Autism

Introduction

I am a veterinarian. I am a woman. I have autism.

Explaining the latter—autism—is like trying to explain color to the color-blind. Autism is a dimension that is outside the realm of normal understanding because it's more in touch with sensory experience than language, which is why neurotypicals (people who do not have autism) cannot fathom it.

There is a reason we're this way. It's because of a place in the brain that doesn't speak; it feels. It's called the limbic system and the amygdala lives there, containing all the emotion you will ever be capable of displaying. It's the place where you love something without words.

It's a place where everything is blended and doesn't require language to make it rational or ordered: it is sensory and feelings only. It's stronger and more intense than language and words. It's where I attach objects to feelings. I'm fairly convinced that autism also lives there, sharing common space with the inability to explain how or what I feel because it's incredibly profound.

Scientific studies show that the amygdala in brains with autism is used more than the frontal lobe, which houses logic, words, and executive thinking. Because those of us who have autism are embedded in a sensory world in our brains, dogs are naturally our mates in life: dogs also have that same leading cognitive function.

For example, dogs sense the coming of lightning, and if they fear it, they will hide. Dogs can sense the approach of an earthquake before the ground trembles. They sense and can warn of an impending seizure or diabetic sugar imbalance. Dogs sense when their owner is sad, happy, or afraid, and they respond accordingly. Dogs *feel*. They don't need it explained to them. They don't care what frightens you; they are there for you. Their response is appropriate. They aren't judgmental and don't demand that you pull yourself

together. They will be silly with you or cuddly, depending on the support you need.

Most dogs don't enjoy loud crowds and noises. They appreciate aversion to sensory overload and prefer quiet walks in the woods compared to farmers' markets, street bazaars, or marching bands. They adapt to the situation and will be your one consistent friend, ready to be outgoing or introverted according to the moment.

I had the rare opportunity to be raised by a father with autism, who understood the necessity of dogs. Before my time, my father was a product of the foster care system: illiterate, unsocial, and defiant. The one thing that kept him grounded and out of trouble when he was younger was his dog, a black Labrador retriever named Queenie. She slept next to him when he was a homeless teenager. She protected him from strangers and wildlife. She was there for him no matter what, and she loved him wholeheartedly. She accepted him every day, consistently, without change or hesitation. She chose him and stayed with him to her death.

When Queenie had groomed my father to be gentle and trusting, she traded her duties to my mother; and Queenie made an excellent choice. My mother is the kindest person on the planet and must have recognized the greatness within him. She taught him to read. He became a successful logger. They are still married and have made a wonderful life and family together, including my older brother, younger brother (who are both "neurotypical"), and me.

Most importantly, my dad recognized something in me that was just like him: I am different from the rest of the world, and I am safe in the presence of a dog. My dad made sure I had a dog my entire life. He understood how important a dog's love and presence could be, so he fostered it.

I didn't have to go to school as a child, because my father, my dog, and I traveled extensively throughout my youth. My father was an innovative entrepreneur who loved to visit interesting destinations, but mostly focused on logging and the timber industry. As a result, I didn't have to comply with the social standards of any culture because I lived in numerous cultures; for example, the tundra of Alaska where the caribou made their treks, the jungles of the Philippines with their indigenous peoples, and with my Native American family at the border of California and Oregon. In the wilderness I could read my books and I could explore with my dog, who protected me and accepted me. Every day. Without hesitation. Without prejudice. Confidence came easily when I had acceptance every day, all day, which is what a dog provides for a person.

Acceptance is the one thing all parents should hope their children achieve, especially their children with autism. It can be used to measure success and, at times, happiness. Even small doses can mean a lot if someone is outside the social norm. To that child, acceptance builds confidence each time it is felt. As valuable as it is, true acceptance doesn't come with that high of a price tag—it comes with a wagging tail and four legs.

I am not a child developmental psychologist. I don't have experience in child rearing. I gained my three stepchildren when the youngest was nine years old, and they are all precocious socially. My knowledge is based on dogs and autism. I can tell you with certainty that any child, but particularly a child with autism, will gain more than can be quantified if he or she has a dog in their home. Any person, neurotypical or not, will blossom in the presence of a dog.

My first dog was Buford, and he was my first brush with a living guardian angel. He obeyed when I called. He stood between me and social interactions, which I didn't understand, and gave me the courage to explore new things. He wasn't a service dog. He was not trained to a special task in helping with a diagnosed disability. He didn't have a formal label of "emotional support animal." He was just our family pet, and he was a pillar of love to me.

Buford came from the shelter—a farm reject because he (allegedly) chased chickens. He was half German shepherd and half Saint Bernard with a size that was intimidating at over 120 pounds. He stood waist-high to most adults and towered over my childhood frame. His coat was thick and mahogany like a giant, fluffy teddy bear. I wrapped my fingers in his coat and slept curled into his flank many times. He was patient and kind. He might not have been cut out for farm work, but he was an exceptional babysitter and I loved him. He accepted me. He wasn't expensive in terms of purchase, though to my family he was priceless. He got me through childhood and set a standard of companionship that I have nourished all my life.

When I first started talking, I talked to Buford. He didn't correct my grammar or pronunciation. He helped me gain confidence in speech. We laughed together and played together. Psychologists would call this a "transition object," something that encouraged a social interaction or dialog that could be eventually used with people. When I first spoke with my cousins, they made fun of me, so I would stop talking for days. In fact, one of my aunts is sure I said no more than four words to her an entire summer while staying at her house.

I used big words for my young age because I was a copious reader, so it wasn't until I was much older that I realized that my cousins didn't understand me, so they were most likely intimidated. Children can be cruel, so I didn't understand them, either. I didn't like their rudeness when I made my attempts to integrate with them.

Buford would never do that to me. He listened, and he was supportive. He, no doubt, got complete sentences and long boring stories that he endured with grace and patience. Once I had years of confidence built up by simulating conversations with Buford, I ventured into the chatty human world and was much more successful. His acceptance gave me confidence. I was practiced, and I knew that I could always go to him if it didn't work out with people or I struggled to find words. Even to this day, I still talk to my dog. They're the easiest conversations I have, filled with respect and honesty. Nothing is dumb or boring; I can ramble or be passionate. I can be accepted.

Talking to a dog is actually a sign of intelligence. Nicholas Epley, a professor of behavioral science at the University of Chicago, has stated that anthropomorphization is what makes humans uniquely more intelligent than animals. Explore communication capacities and show off autism's brilliance by interacting with a dog and, perhaps, your

dog will get you (or your child) through childhood and set a standard of companionship that will nourish a lifetime.

As I gained more verbal acuity, I got to experience more types of dogs. For many females on the autism spectrum, language is not always our paramount struggle; as a result, our diagnoses can be overlooked for a long time. My diagnosis came as an adult. Until then, I had many dogs to help me transition into the world and into my profession as a veterinarian. Although my childhood might sound lonely to some, I was never alone. I always had my dog and my father, who understood and loved me. Loneliness is an illness. It is sadness and self-perpetuating. It has been linked to an exaggerated level of interleukin 6 (IL-6), which is an immune protein found in depressed individuals.

Interestingly, it is not found in any measurable amounts in those raised in a rural setting with dogs. In fact, *Newsweek* recently published an article by Kate Sheridan suggesting that childhood pets can make people mentally healthier and proved this correlation with the levels of IL-6 in those raised on a farm compared to those from metropolitan areas. It is not a definitive mental health prescription and is still in early research, but if it were that simple—this one thing with so many benefits—you would surely consider getting a dog. They aren't as expensive as therapies, pills, doctors' visits, and counseling, which are tied to loneliness, sadness, and frustration for many children. There are so few reasons not to get yourself or your family a dog, and so many wonderful possibilities in doing so.

Chapter 1

Buy a Dog!

Y ou don't have to buy a $3,000 designer breed puppy and worry about training and socializing it properly. Most of my childhood dogs were from shelters. The shelter fee for adoption includes the spay/neuter and first year's vaccinations. There are usually free puppy classes or programs sponsored by rescue groups that you can attend to gain skills to train the dog and overcome any problems integrating your new puppy into the home.

Most adult dogs come already housebroken and leash trained. As far as costs go, they may need grooming—depending on the breed—occasional veterinary visits, and obviously, food.

If that sounds daunting, consider that pet owners are 0.6 times less likely to visit their own doctors due to illnesses. This may be due to dog walking, which has been shown to help lose weight, lower triglycerides, delay dementia, and increase relaxation. Additionally, dogs have been able to calm anxiety, decrease heart rate, and drop blood

pressure just by their presence alone. The American Heart Association has provided many articles on these benefits, with hard statistics supporting lower cardiovascular risk and better recovery post-heart attack for dog owners. Your medical bills could be lower by owning a dog. It's symbiotic. And it's so much cheaper than hippotherapy.

Hippotherapy, the therapeutic use of horseback riding, has various positive attributes. Many types of social difficulties that are problematic for those on the autism spectrum can be breached by interaction with a horse. The biophilia hypothesis is real: humans have an innate requirement to connect with nature. It brings out a feeling of fulfillment and balance. Having a dog in the home increases these interactions with animals from a weekly event, which is the usual pattern for horseback riding, to a constant daily presence. Your or your child can choose to interact or not interact with a dog. Unlike a scheduled event at horse camp, where the person interacts with the horse for a limited period of time, a dog's presence can be ignored or cherished depending on the mood from one moment to the next. There are no expensive handlers, no car rides to the countryside or a stable to spend time with your dog. The dog is willing and able at a moment's notice to provide love and companionship because he's right there at your feet.

What's the Worst That Could Happen? Being Bitten?

What's the worst that could happen? Are you afraid the dog may bite? I have worked in the veterinary field for twenty-two years, ten of that as an emergency veterinarian, and I have never been bitten. I see dogs at their absolute worst: hit by cars, attacked by other dogs, porcupine encounters, illnesses, accidental poisonings, and all manner of injuries. I have to touch them, find the problem, and sometimes carry them when they are broken and painful. I have never been bitten. I see twenty to forty patients a day that are hurt, scared, and unfamiliar, and I have never been bitten. I'm not saying your child won't get bitten, but I can say that it is highly unlikely. And there is data to support it.

There are 70 million dogs in America. Only about 4.5 million have reported dog bites of which half are children, and only one in five require medical attention. Unfortunately, most dog bites are within the family, not strays or stranger-owned. Commonly, it's boys and toddlers that look dogs in the eye. People with autism do not generally like direct eye contact and are, therefore, less likely to bring out the "challenge stare" in a dog when making their introduction. Face-to-face contact (such as cheek-to-cheek, not nose-to-nose) is also relatively low on the bite list, as long as the child is below the dog. This may be due to the wolf interaction, in which the omega pack members bite at the lower jaw of the alpha members showing submission. The dog may be domesticated, but he is still a canine, and many social patterns are still strong in the family hound.

Slow blinking and turning away also reduces the aggressive response in dogs, which happened to be my go-to method of avoiding social interactions when I was younger.

In general, dogs are predictable. They have very consistent tolerances and are quick to pick up on non-verbal cues like nervousness and hesitance. They rarely force interaction, and when they do, they don't care what kind of response they get as long as it's attention. They don't judge too harshly and are not biased in any way. They will accept kindness from just about anybody and return it with gusto.

Do Your Research on Breeds and Know Their Natural History

To reduce the likelihood of a bite, choose a pet dog wisely. Do your research and try to balance a dog with the lifestyle and household it will be living in. When everybody is happy, there is less opportunity for biting. Statistically speaking, small dogs under twenty pounds are less likely to bite compared to dogs over fifty pounds.

Do your research on breeds and know their natural history. The American Kennel Club (AKC) and most of your brand-name dog food companies have fun online algorithms that can help you narrow down the search criteria to specific breeds compatible with your family régime. Certain breeds of dogs are more aggressive by nature than others, so there is a more inherent risk. One just has to reflect on the golden retriever and the German shepherd to make an accurate assumption: in the population of goldens, there are fewer biters than in the shepherd group. The original primitive purpose of the dog comes into play. The golden retriever was bred to assist the fowl hunter by patiently waiting at his side until instructed to fetch. It is to have a soft mouth to gently retrieve a delicate bird without bruising or damaging the meat. It is patient and kind—never rushing its prey, only waiting for it to fall by the hand of the hunter. The German shepherd is bred to protect and herd goats and sheep with minimal human oversight; it will work independently. It is an aggressive motivator to get the entire flock moving or to shoo away a potential predator. It does not take "no" or hesitance for an answer and will quickly bite at its flock to get a large population moving. Shepherds are known to fight wolves and coyotes to preserve the vulnerable members of their charge. There is a saying that "the sheep fear their sheepdog/shepherd because they have seen his teeth when he fights the wolves." Though he is designed to be their protector, he is first a fighter.

Animal domestication occurred at the beginning of man's walk on the earth, starting with the dog/wolf. The wolf had a use because he could provide food and would also offer protection. Over the years, tameness was selected into the wolf-now-dog, which can be replicated

in breeding fur-bearing foxes within just a few generations. Farms that raise foxes have realized that they are quick to domesticate by simply selecting individuals that do not growl when their cage is opened. After just two or three generations, none of the foxes growl when approached and can be reasonably described as friendly. They are still foxes, and it would take centuries to make them into a dog, but they can be safe to handle. Selection and purpose-breeding is a phenomenon that can be easily exploited for man's wishes. As more diversified survival tactics developed in the genesis of time, the dog learned to adapt and branched into herding breeds, livestock guardians, deer hunters, bird hunters, rat hunters, and the tiny, simple companion.

A Dog Bred to Run and Kill Isn't a Good Choice for an Apartment

A dog that has been bred for millennia to hunt and kill wolves is not a good choice for apartment living. One cannot expect that a few hundred years of breeding will eliminate the desire to run and kill. The dog's expectations for exercise and play may not match well with an owner whose job that takes them out of the home eight to ten hours a day, five days a week.

No wonder some pet owners come home to shredded couches and soiled carpets! Boredom is dangerous and can be considered a breed-specific problem in many cases.

Biting can also be considered a breed-specific problem in many cases. Dogs bred to fight each other or fight other animals can make good pets, but there are literally thousands of years of breeding that makes them bite, so turning that mechanism off is not as simple as a loving home. Over 60 percent of all fatal attacks are committed by breeds lumped into the pit bull category: American Staffordshire terriers, American bully, Staffordshire bull terrier and, occasionally, the American bulldog. One person's loving pet may not work well for someone else. Once again, choose wisely.

The average dog will give warnings before biting, and it is up to the handlers to recognize his or her limitations. For some dogs, that boundary is very easily breached. Since it is consistent, it can be a pattern a person with autism can easily learn and remember. There are no facial cues to decipher and no voice inflections you have to translate as you do with people who might be ready to attack. The non-aggressive dog will move away, give warning, and then bite when cornered.

The degree of stimulation to reach biting varies highly with each individual dog and the degree of pressure you place on him, which can be mostly age dependent. A puppy may be a good choice so that they can grow up with your family, but they do require more training and patience the first year.

Getting a grown dog from another family can turn out well, too. Some dogs are not good fits for the home they were originally chosen for, but they can be ideal housemates in another. Just because someone doesn't want the dog doesn't necessarily mean the dog is a failure. It's all about pairing up the right combination. An old dog may have arthritis and will not be as forgiving to rough handling or play. It could become a biter when its pain overwhelms its reasoning. On the other hand, it could be already well-trained and patient. Think of it as an interview process for a soul mate. It's not about the money you will spend, but the right addition to your home that brings joy and fulfillment.

There is no perfect breed of dog. So many families choose those they have had experience with as a child or young adult, but any dog can be the ideal companion in the right circumstance. Forty-four percent of American households just can't be wrong. Rarely have I seen a mismatched pair of dog and person, and when I do, it usually is no fault

of the dog. People occasionally have unrealistic goals and/ or lousy training skills. There are also movies that influence a lot of prejudicial expectations (thank you, *Lassie*, *Rin Tin Tin*, and *Benji*), which no dog could reasonably fulfill. There could be a different dog out there that would complement the family nicely. So, try the dog, but be realistic. If it doesn't work out, try another. There should be no hard feelings when you part ways. Think of it as a dating process until you find the one and only. There's a match out there for every household. When you see it work correctly, your heart will melt. The dog will sit quietly, allowing touch if he wants or enjoying time to just be with you. He (or she) accepts whatever social interaction the person is capable or willing to give. He won't ask for more, he won't give any less. He just accepts. No words, no demands, no conditions. A dog's acceptance is always complete and honest. He is there consistently and is never inconvenienced by schedules or phones or life outside that very moment. He demands nothing in return. There is no other social interaction that even closely resembles the kindness and support a dog's unconditional love proves. It is a safe place to be. When a child is safe and comfortable, she can learn and grow with eagerness. When an adult is comfortable, social interactions like work and life outside the home can be accomplished seamlessly. People of all ages, especially people on the autism spectrum, can flourish by adding a dog to their home.

Communication with dogs is not always about words, which is a breath of fresh air for most people with autism. Communication can be touch, nonverbal, or just pure emotion. Sometimes you need someone to be there for you; a non-judgmental, non-inquisitive soul to have your back. There are times that I am flooded with feelings and/or have sensory overload and can't explain why I'm sad or angry or happy. It is frustrating when a person needs an explanation of your emotional position before he feels he can understand it or comfort you. A dog is different. The dog will share your emotion and not ask questions. She will bounce around and be happy when playfulness is warranted or can be quiet and cuddly when you need a shoulder to lean on. Acceptance is so darn hard, and yet, it comes easily to a dog. She asks for no explanations. Whatever you want or need, she accepts you. She accepts autism. She accepts whatever life throws her way. A dog's love and acceptance are so empowering! I have witnessed it every day of

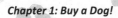

my own life and every day in the lives of others as a veterinarian. Owning a dog is truly life-changing.

I was raised with many types and sizes of dogs, and I learned early on that they speak my language. Dogs speak autism. I understand them, and they understand me. You owe to yourself (or your child) dialogue that is unconstrained, companionship that lacks social protocol, communication without words, and above all, acceptance—which is a dog's greatest gift to the world.

Chapter 2

Human-Animal Bond:
The Science is There

Courtrooms nationwide have adopted the use of dogs to bring comfort to victims during stressful trials. Dogs have been recognized for their positivity in hospitals, hospice-care settings, and nursing homes. There are legitimate facts proving that elderly individuals are healthier and live longer when they have a dog. Dogs calm our fears.

When there were several incidents of violence at my daughter's university, the chancellor brought in golden retriever puppies for the students to play with for several days. Their benefits are not anecdotal, they exist. Dogs make your life better.

Dogs Beget Healing, Literally!

Science has documented an increase in the oxytocin hormone during positive interactions with dogs. Oxytocin is important for stimulating social bonding, relaxation, and trust; therefore, it eases stress. Other hormones that get a boost with dog interactions are dopamine (the "happy hormone"), phenylethylamine (responsible for the feeling of elation), and prolactin (nurturing). Additionally, cortisol goes down, meaning the overall stress and the harmful anxiety that goes with it is reduced. My favorite benefit is not hormonal—it's part of the nervous system, a portion of the system that defines people with autism as different than others.

Dogs influence the unconscious function of heart rate, metabolism, and healing modulated by the vagus nerve system. Hugging a dog can stimulate the vagus nerve system in a positive way. Petting a dog can actually increase energy storage and promote growth and healing. The vagus nerve system can be engaged by the comforting smell of the pet's fur, the sound of its paws dancing across the floor, and the softness of its fur. This all culminates in a positive effect upon sensory and emotional needs, which is exactly what any person—particularly a person with autism—needs.

The healing power of dogs may be explained by modern science with fancy words, chemical analysis, and nerve conduction tests, but

people have intuitively known that it was true long before it was proven. The ancient Egyptians believed that dog saliva cured infections and allowed them to lick human wounds; we now know that there are actually some antibacterial and antiviral substances in the saliva of dogs. The Egyptians rewarded the dog by treating them like family, burying over eight million dog mummies in their precious tombs. The cat may have been an unreachable god to them, never fully domesticated, but it never achieved the honorary title of "man's best friend." The cat was placed on a pedestal, it wasn't part of the family. It didn't reciprocate love and affection in the same way as a dog. The cat provided not much more than companionship, the dog is scientifically beneficial to wellbeing.

The nineteenth-century nurse Florence Nightingale wrote that a small pet "is often an excellent companion for the sick, for long chronic cases especially." She understood the value of a dog and the unexplainable benefits of its presence. She is often considered the founder of modern nursing, but her very first patient was a dog named Cap. Her success and satisfaction with helping him when she was a child led her to pursue a greater vocation during many wars and throughout many countries. She changed the lives of literally thousands of individuals and influenced the lives of many, even to this day. Never underestimate the power of a simple interaction with a dog. It can truly be life-changing.

Dogs have also reduced the incidence of allergies and asthma during childhood years. It is based on the "hygiene hypothesis," which suggests that a less-than-clean environment in childhood can reduce the occasions of hay fever and other maladies by exposing one's immune system to a wide range of challenges in the early developmental years. If you do develop a peanut allergy, there are dogs specifically trained to intervene when you are about to be exposed to them to save your life. Dogs can also be trained to diagnose cancer in early stages. They seem to have innate senses regarding the safety and wellbeing of their humans.

There is no limit to their ability to please their owners by learning new things. That's why we have working dogs in so many fields: cadaver search, tracking, police, herding, guiding the blind, sniffing for bed bugs, hunting, and guarding. Probably the most appreciated is the therapy dog, the kind companion that has been well socialized, well trained, and is willing to interact with all manner of individuals. She is seen in hospitals, airports, and nursing homes, providing magical benefits via her presence and kindness. A therapy dog's value exceeds the cost of training and purchase; her virtue is akin to an angel, blessing her charges with unspeakable love.

Many individuals experiencing post-traumatic stress syndrome acquire dogs to mitigate feelings of inadequacy and suicide. There are large national organizations working to put dogs in homes with postwar veterans and the elderly. The differences in mental and physical health are not always clear; the brain is a wondrous organ, and illness can truly be "all in our head" but clinically manifest in the body. A dog is there to act as a loving and accepting friend that asks for nothing in return except for a kind pat, a safe place to rest, and a reliable food source. He won't care if you're clinically unstable, emotionally drained, or socially awkward. He's there for you when you need him. For millennia, dogs have served their masters with loyalty and love, even when it may not have been reciprocated or deserved.

The world knows how important dogs are. It recognizes and respects the human-animal bond with its generous benefits. Nepal thanks dogs every year in a festival recognizing the dog's service, loyalty, and love. Socrates claimed that the dog is a true philosopher because dogs "distinguish the face of a friend and of an enemy only by the criterion of knowing and not knowing." He concludes that dogs must be lovers of learning because they determine what they like and what they do not based upon knowledge of the truth. There is no deception or ambiguity in their friendship, they will trust and love until proven unsafe to do so. Their affection is not influenced by peer pressure, media, or other aspects of the unfathomable social world of neurotypicals.

The human-animal bond is a well-documented and greatly discussed phenomena that the veterinary field has long recognized. Many articles in the *Journal of the American Veterinary Medical Association* have touted the responsibility of veterinarians to recognize and respect the bond, not just for a successful practice but for successful interactions with clients and patients. It clearly states that the veterinarian's role is to maximize the potentials of this relationship between people and animals as it is mutually beneficial and dynamic. Animals can influence behaviors essential to the health and wellbeing of each other and their people. We love our dogs, and they love us back. The bond is real and powerful. Purdue University College of Veterinary Medicine has established the Center for the Human-Animal Bond, which is committed to expanding the knowledge of interrelationships between animals and their environment. As a veterinarian, I was eager to get my human-animal bond certification, but I must say that I recognized long before becoming a veterinarian that the bond was very powerful and real. It greatly improved my interactions with people and reduced anxiety, and can undoubtedly do the same for your child with autism.

Amazingly, dogs make social interaction look easy without excluding those that struggle with the concept. Dogs are outgoing. It's hard not to tag along with them. They make friends easily and are not judgmental or discriminatory. They teach us that it is okay to be different. They are happy to go along with whomever to wherever. They don't even have to know where they are going, they are just pleased to be included on the ride.

Their language is mostly sensory, too. They store their data based on previous experiences but seem to lack the general fear of the unknown that most people on the autism spectrum foster. They engage effortlessly. My current personal dog is well-versed in this phenomenon.

She's four pounds of poodle, dyed multiple colors (safely and with non-toxic product!) depending on the season at hand: pink for Valentine's Day, green for Saint Patrick's Day, patriotic colors for the 4th of July, and so forth. She is a social butterfly and assumes everyone adores her—probably because everyone does, and she has never had a bad experience to make her consider otherwise. In public, everyone wants to pet her and comment on her color of the month. She has a fan club and a Facebook following. She's exactly the kind of social prima donna that, in a human, I would not understand. She fits her name, Bazinga.

Having her is a diversion that helps me transition into everyday conversation with strangers. Most interactions skip the tedious "How are you?" and go straight to "Your dog is adorable. Can I pat her?" Which, of course, Bazinga readily obliges. Their questions are easily answered: "What's her name?" "Why is she colored orange and green?" "What kind of dog is she?" Each question is logical and has a definitive answer, which is not attached to a great deal of sensory questions often addressed to me, like "What are your plans for today?" or "How is your day going?" These kinds of questions stir instant anxiety and emotion on my part, so I may not have a rational answer. I don't want to share my plans. Maybe I don't have any plans. Maybe I have to look at my appointment book to determine where I'm headed in the next twenty minutes. Do I say this? Do I lie? How is my day? Aside from subject to entropy, it's the same as any other day. It travels at the same speed as yours. It's going around in twenty-three hours, fifty-six minutes and four seconds with an orbital rotation of 460 meters per second. Why did you ask?

Your dog may help your child make friends with the neighbors. People may engage your child while she is out walking the dog, and the friendliness of the dog can provide confidence and a topic the child may easily talk about. Bazinga helps me achieve social acceptance because my limitations are usually masked by her charm. Everyone wants to engage the dog and forget the handler. A person with a dog is accepted and engaged easily; for a person who has autism, the leash is a bridge between awkward, forced interactions to confidence. Attention is diverted to the dog, so conversation is triangular with the dog, not direct and intimidating. Additionally, subtle non-confrontational

postures are unknowingly exhibited by the neurotypical when a child has a dog on the leash: kneeling to the dog and child's level, less intimidating eye contact because the dog receives the majority of the attention, a softer tone of voice, and a lack of sudden gestures. Usually, the dog is situated between the person and child, giving the child a sense of safety behind a comforting presence. The dog encourages further interactions, building on positive experiences. Psychologists emphasize the importance of repeated, positive stimuli to make the extinction of fear possible. Your child could become bolder and more likely to talk by using the dog as common ground. Remember that fear and anxiety are different. Fear is a memory of an actual event similar to the current circumstances that were unpleasant, painful, or harmful. It is not your call to say whether or not it's lucid; it's a personal perspective and real to that person who has problems socializing. That's why desensitization can work. When positive experiences outnumber negative, the overwhelming emotion is no longer adverse. Fear can be destroyed. Anxiety, however, is different. Repeated exposure doesn't always change the perception of an anxious person. Anxiety is the emotion that is attached to perceived danger. It's the brain thinking something could possibly be bad with no direct experience to prove otherwise. It's the idea of danger, wherein the mind heads down several different roads and loses rationality along the way. This derailment is not easily repaired, because there is no history to pair outcomes.

Both fear and anxiety trigger the fight or flight response, the switch from which there is no return. Adrenaline and epinephrine flood the neurologic system and reason is overwhelmed. This also includes the newly described "amygdala hijack," with its overwhelming and immediate response to stimuli that is out of proportion to the threat. Remember that autism lives in the amygdala. It is surrounded by sensory and emotion with no language to release it. That's why our reaction to stimuli is not perceived as reasonable to neurotypicals; it's quick and exaggerated. A neurotypical would have no idea how we have stored our previous information and it may not be the most "sensible" pathway. To us, it's where we live. It is the only response. It is our way. Telling us to fix it doesn't change it. Reducing our fear modulates it, so give us a bridge to reduce our fear. Give us confidence and we can lengthen the fuse to extreme response. Give us a dog and he will calm our fears.

As a practicing veterinarian, I can interact with the dog and, therefore, interact with people while portraying a perfectly seamless grasp of sociality—which really doesn't exist. I don't have to understand the entire human conversation because I can see the bond and I can understand the dog. I can make a difference, since the bond gives me a bridge to common ground and communication. There can be a lot of feelings involved when a sick dog is presented to me, but it is the one time that I understand neurotypical fears. I live in the same emotional warehouse, we just need to find common stock to get it organized. The bond is sensory and emotional and is without language. I don't need to use words to understand it because I feel it, too.

The value of a dog is so much more than the price of care. It is more than love and companionship. It is acceptance and contentment and happiness, all things without measure, and most importantly, without words. The value of canine companionship cannot be overstated.

Chapter 3

Multiple Dogs, Breed Size, and More!

When I was younger, I felt small. The world was large and the people in it were overbearing. I wanted to hide. I was fearful of the unknown (and, occasionally, the known). Buford saved me from internalizing that fear. He was not a small dog, he was many times my weight and size and he didn't fear anything. I am pretty sure just about everything feared him. To my four-year-old frame, he was a doting bear and a pony I often rode. He did not allow strangers to approach me and, literally, stood between me and the world. His presence was intimidating if you didn't know him and comforting if you did. He represented both the feared monster and the sanctuary.

He established my understanding of dogs and the human-animal bond. I saw him barking in the back of my dad's service truck when a stranger approached too closely; he appeared vicious and as if he were about to leap from the truck to the person. Because my dog didn't trust him, this stranger surely must be untrustworthy. Buford positioned himself between me and the world, and I was thankful. I was bonded to him and it opened my eyes to the bond others have with their dogs. I knew my dog would not let other people approach and that their dogs would do the same for them. I could stand behind Buford so his whole body would obscure me, protecting me from the social world in which I struggled. I was empowered by his protection and spoke to him often. He was not outgoing to strangers and would guide me away from interactions. His size was a comfort to me when I needed a guardian, any smaller and he would not have had the same effect on approaching strangers. Any more social and he would have left me to integrate on my own. He was the perfect combination of strength and security.

There were times when his size was cumbersome. Taking him places required a truck, and he abhorred the indoors. He was well suited for the cold: he had a thick coat that repelled the snow and remained fluffy, despite rare grooming. For his job, he was the perfect match. He guarded my dad's property (me included) and never roamed. He was there to comfort me. I learned to be brave with his presence, which empowered me as I grew bigger. If I had been a less-verbal person, I think this type of dog would have been the perfect match throughout my life. He tolerated cuddles and I often slept nestled into his fur. He listened when I jabbered and was sympathetic to my meltdowns. He made me realize my love for dogs and helped me recognize that I need one at all times. I felt loved and safe when I was with him, and I was less anxious socially. If you were to search for a dog of his caliber, you would have to consider a Newfoundland, Great Pyrenees, Anatolian shepherd, Leonberger, giant schnauzer, or Saint Bernard. They were originally developed for livestock guarding and are attentive to their flock or family. They require minimal exercise and are content with their job as a massive presence overseeing their charge. They have thick, fluffy coats to protect them from the cold and attack from predators (a need that has luckily become antiquated). They will shed often with minimal grooming. Most in this category weigh over 100 pounds and stand thirty to thirty-six inches at the shoulder. As an adult, you can pet them without bending over. They are not socially outgoing and usually remain standoffish but not aggressive. Many people find them difficult to read (or understand) because they do not exhibit the typical tail wag and eagerness to engage with strangers. They are calculating and therefore perfect for a less-verbal child with autism—these breeds will take everything in with calmness and reason.

The talents of your dog are not always dependent on his size or breeding. I have seen Boston terriers perform agility trails and Pomeranians contend in frisbee meets. Your dog is unique to your home. You can buy a puppy from the same breed of dog nine times and have nine very different individuals. They are as different as people on this planet. I have had four tiny toy poodles and four Labrador retrievers in my lifetime, and they each brought something very different to my life when I needed it the most. Their lives overlapped, but their talents did not. The personalities were never similar, so their level of play and learning were also highly variable. The wealth of love and wisdom I gained from each cannot be measured.

Personalities are quite broad in the dog world and more diverse than size and breed. Breed size does matter, though, and I would recommend pairing a fifty- to eighty-pound dog with small children, so they can have a presence to stand behind as I did when I was younger.

Depending on your family, having more than one dog in the home should be fine—especially if they are personality diverse. Their interactions can be entertaining and a source of enlightenment. They can have their separate roles with a combined goal: helping your child blossom socially. Having more than two dogs can be a distraction, and I would not recommend it in a home with a child with autism. You want the dogs' attention on the child and do not want them to develop a pack mentality. Your dog's routine should be all about your child. One dog is awesome, but more is not necessarily better.

Having a small dog and a big dog at the same time requires the perfect combination of individuals, because a large dog can put the entire body of the small dog in its mouth and do some serious harm in a moment. Generally, having the small dog first and introducing the large dog as a puppy guarantees the hierarchy maintains respect for the little guy throughout both their lifetimes. Having dogs of various sizes gives you options. Tiny dogs are portable. Big dogs like to go jogging and tag along during horseback rides. Tiny dogs sleep on the bed. Large dogs guard the house at night. Tiny dogs can be taken in a backpack or purse to social events. Large dogs make a presence that a child can hide behind when frightened or uncertain.

Having multiple dogs does have benefits; they keep each other company if they cannot be with me. They can be separated, and when they are reunited, they greet each other with tail wags and kisses. There is no animosity because one got to go and the other stayed. They are kind to one another and happy to share our lives.

If you do opt to have more than one dog, it is okay to have a favorite. Bazinga is the favorite, and she knows it. Her dog housemates know it. Favoritism is harmless and normal. I have a bond with all of my dogs, it's just stronger with Bazinga. She spends more time with me, which increases the bond. It is a self-perpetuating phenomenon. She is the only dog allowed to sleep on the bed or get onto the furniture. She takes the other dogs' toys up there, because she knows they cannot take them back. She is spicy and spoiled, and yet absolutely adorable. Just be sure you interact with all your animals daily.

You may not be ready to have two dogs at the same time, and that's okay. Just try not to let the gaps between dogs become too lengthy. A dog is good for physical and mental health. He can help you heal and grow and he prevents loneliness. Our homes are warmer with dogs as a part of them. Copacetic. All is right with the world.

Retriever Size

A retriever has a size that can be intimidating to others, but most importantly, it can faithfully stand between a child and a stranger. Two feet tall at the shoulder is plenty big enough to protect a child. A retriever is not the scary guardian of the giant breeds (over 100 pounds)

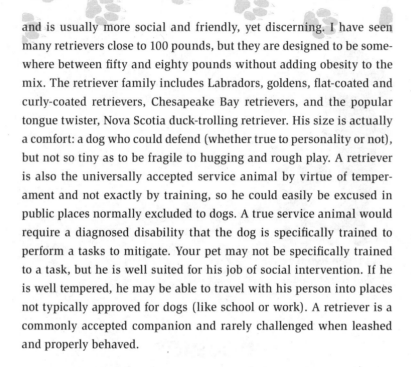

and is usually more social and friendly, yet discerning. I have seen many retrievers close to 100 pounds, but they are designed to be somewhere between fifty and eighty pounds without adding obesity to the mix. The retriever family includes Labradors, goldens, flat-coated and curly-coated retrievers, Chesapeake Bay retrievers, and the popular tongue twister, Nova Scotia duck-trolling retriever. His size is actually a comfort: a dog who could defend (whether true to personality or not), but not so tiny as to be fragile to hugging and rough play. A retriever is also the universally accepted service animal by virtue of temperament and not exactly by training, so he could easily be excused in public places normally excluded to dogs. A true service animal would require a diagnosed disability that the dog is specifically trained to perform a tasks to mitigate. Your pet may not be specifically trained to a task, but he is well suited for his job of social intervention. If he is well tempered, he may be able to travel with his person into places not typically approved for dogs (like school or work). A retriever is a commonly accepted companion and rarely challenged when leashed and properly behaved.

Moderately Sized Dogs

Other dog breeds of moderate size include spaniels, terriers, and shepherds. They weigh about thirty to fifty pounds and stand less than two feet at the shoulder, some even as small as eight inches. There are twenty-five types of spaniels, thirty terriers, and twenty-eight shepherds to choose from. The American Kennel Club has divided them up into their distinct classifications (show groups) which include sporting, non-sporting, working, and herding. There is sure to be a match that fits your household. These breeds typically require more training and activity to stymie boredom and the occasional destructive

Less than two feet tall at the shoulder

behavior associated with it. Playing fetch and long walks are proactive and may help a child gain confidence and skills. For example, while walking a dog, many people will make small talk directed to the pet, which may help the child transition into conversation. Questions about the dog are easier to answer than questions regarding the child. They also have simple answers that don't inflict social anxiety like "How are you?" which does not have a rational answer because you're expected to have a canned answer. "What's your dog's name?" has a rational answer. Most people with autism like to talk about our passions and interests, which could definitely include our dogs.

Beagles

Charles M. Schulz wrote the cartoon script about Charlie Brown and his dog, Snoopy. His depiction of canine companionship established an entire generation of beagle-loving individuals. Loyalty, love, and laughter, all the joys of childhood wrapped into a twenty-pound ball of fur. The beagle is a good size, not too big and not too small. He can be fierce and an obnoxious barker. Even Snoopy was known to say, "I feel like a can of mace!" Overall, a beagle is a reliable companion. He is a hound and can be a house

dog, trained to many imaginable tricks. Known to be both smart and stubborn, he may need an experienced owner to bring out the finest qualities of his breeding. He could be a good match for a myriad of human social inadequacies, including shyness (the beagle will not let you hide alone!), non-verbal (he can do a lot of "talking" for you), and outbursts. I've known beagles to howl when their owner's children cry until they are brought to laughter. It's a strange paradigm but very common. Dogs, certainly including beagles, are really in tune with emotion and feelings. They want to fix it with their exorbitance of happiness and love.

Boxers

Another great family dog is the boxer. Though the breed in general may face some health problems (cancer, heart disease, hypothyroidism, hip dysplasia, eye and neurologic diseases including epilepsy), individuals can be robust and fun. They are active and playful, averaging about two feet at the shoulder and forty to sixty pounds. They require very little training and can be content as apartment dogs with daily walks, or as active frisbee champions. They are of a large size and can be good guardians and watchdogs. The best description of a boxer is "silly," they have a wrinkly, happy face and outgoing personalities.

Newfoundlands

An even larger dog is the Newfoundland, who is not much of an athlete but could benefit from good exercise like any mammal. She would be an excellent choice for a child who is a little bit of a homebody and needs more than moral support to initiate interaction. The Newfoundland is famous for water rescue and is very patient due to her tolerance of many boring days on ships (historically). She can live in a small space comparable to her stature and requires minimal training. She is the presence that gives comfort and confidence by physically standing between autism and the rest of the world, protecting the child from danger both real and imagined. She is well suited for children of all ages and can reduce shyness by giving a child a safety barrier not easily breached. The Newfoundland does a good job of rising to the challenge at 100 to 150 pounds and more than twenty-eight inches at the shoulder.

Pugs, Wheaten Terriers, Bichon Frise, and the Dachshund

Good choices of smaller dogs in the twenty-pound category are pugs (that is, if you don't mind wheezing and snoring), Brussels griffon, the soft-coated wheaten terrier, the bichon frise, and the dachshund. Advocates for each breed will tote the merits of their choice to sway allegiance, but keep in mind that each household has a unique circumstance and position to be filled that more than one type may complete or complement. It is, after all, your choice.

The Perfect Dog

There are over 300 breeds of dog in the world, and 192 recognized at the American Kennel Club. As a veterinarian, many people ask me, "What breed is the perfect dog?" Personally, I believe the poodle is the closest there can be to a perfect breed. Sometimes I say "the poodle," and sometimes I opt to let them figure it out on their own. From everything I've learned, the true "perfect dog" is the dog that fits your lifestyle.

When I recommend a poodle, I have a long dissertation of reasons that I'm sure instigates instant regret in the recipient for asking. The virtues of poodle ownership pour from deep within me; I am some-times shocked by the fascinating and numerous merits of the breed.

The poodle comes in any size or color you can imagine: toy (less than five pounds and under ten inches at the shoulder); miniature (about fifteen pounds and no more than thirty-eight inches tall); and standard (about fifty pounds and over thirty-eight inches); white, black, various shades of chocolate, red and blond with solid or patchy coats or party colors, or silvers/greys with highlights, too.

Don't let their light weight fool you. A standard poodle stands taller than an eighty-pound Labrador, even though the poodle weighs about half as much! Her size can be a formable presence when she chooses and a barrier to social interactions. She is also much more athletic than a spaniel or Labrador—gazelle-like, actually—and re-trieves pheasants and ducks while hunting, which, I might add, is another redeemable quality of the poodle: they are versatile. Therapy dog, hunting dog, guard dog, and lap hound—poodles qualify for all!

Poodles are hypoallergenic and do not shed. You can have a long-coated dog, short-coated, corded (like dreadlocks), or any combi-nation you desire. You can clip their coat into any style of your choos-ing and even color it! I've seen poodles groomed to look like zebras, lions, pandas, and pink apparitions. They can be tiny and highly por-table, allowing you to tuck them into a purse-like carrying bag, or they can be large and protective. I have one of each: tiny Bazinga at four pounds of attitude and forty-two-pound Grace, who is slow to make friends but quick to go hunting. When I take Grace to work with me, she won't let anyone near my truck or office. She barks and growls and has been known to actually bite when cornered in our home by a house guest she did not recognize (who let himself in while we were away at work). Bazinga demands to be the center of attention and, though she does not have the dominant presence that Grace has, she can be quite insistent for affection, jumping at your legs until you pet her or pick her up.

Poodles are even-tempered. Ever hear of a person attacked by a poodle? Does a pack of poodles make the headlines for terrorizing a neighborhood? No! Poodles are loved and cherished. They rarely make it to shelters and, when they do, they are adopted promptly. They can be trained in agility, allergy alert, and assistance to the blind as a seeing-eye dog. They are long-lived and exceptionally healthy. Across all breeds of dogs, their stillborn rate and early neonatal mortality are the lowest. They are not prone to genetic diseases or defects. There is not another breed of dog with so many fine characteristics and qualities. I've seen them as tiny companions to the elderly and devoted guard dogs at residences. They could be your jogging companion or your couch potato. Learning tricks is the epitome of poodle behavior, they flourish with training. Of all the dogs I see as a veterinarian, rarely do I meet a disagreeable poodle. They are so treasured that an entire culture of crossbreeds has developed: the labradoodle, goldendoodle, and so many other "doodles," all of half-poodle origin.

Poodles were the dogs of royalty since before King Louis the XVI and were in fifteenth-century portraits as the traditional dog of the time. They are one of the most ancient of breeds, influencing the development of many others including schnauzers, bichons, and similar small, white, fluffy dogs. They were status symbols of the upper class during the founding of the Kennel Club and one of the first breeds to be registered in the 1870s. Their intelligence is ranked second behind the border collie, and they require very specific training or will problem solve on their own. During World War II, poodles assisted the military in a program known as "Dogs for Defense." They were literally an entire group of overachievers doing the jobs of all the other breeds with grace and poise. Pointer? Yep, got that. Water dog? No problem! Status symbol? With the best hairdo ever! Accessory? Toy size, at your service!

They are absolutely suitable for any task presented. If, for some reason, you do not see the merits of poodle ownership, venture to another breed of dog to populate your home. There are fine choices in all groups, and you won't be disappointed.

If You're a Frequent Traveler

If you expect to travel or attend events with your child, I would suggest a smaller sized dog because he is more transportable. Small dogs are usually classified as anything under twenty pounds, but can be further divided into "small" and "toy." A dog of fifteen to twenty pounds like the beagle, Cavalier King Charles spaniel, miniature schnauzer, Jack Russell terrier, or bichon frise can be carried, but they are cumbersome. If you don't like hair in your backpack, consider the Chinese crested (mostly hairless), whippet, or Boston terrier. Dogs under ten pounds, even so much as four pounds, are very unobtrusive. A well-behaved dog of any size is usu-ally welcome, but one that can be tucked into a purse or sweatshirt is often overlooked and mostly never challenged. The toy breeds are ideal for this since they are usually under ten pounds and include fluffy individuals like the Havanese, Maltese, Pomeranian, Yorkshire terrier, papillon, and poodle. You can also get a short-coated variety like the Chihuahua, miniature pincher, or toy fox terrier that would tolerate fun clothing like sweaters and t-shirts. For my entire adult life, I have taken a toy poodle with me literally everywhere.

I have autism, so she is my coping mechanism. My truck is explicitly modified to lock with the air conditioning or heat running and has food and water readily available if the poodle cannot enter the building with me for some reason. She can go to work with me at the veterinary emergency clinic, where she has a bed in my office and a designated chair in the treatment area. My staff accommodates her and she loves them. I am safe with her presence. I can hug her when I'm sad or challenged. I can talk to her. She gets me through the day. During my college career, my poodle went to class every day tucked into my sweatshirt. I don't think anyone actually noticed, or, if they did, they didn't challenge it. The poodle was well behaved, quiet, and content to be next to me. It was symbiotic. I am not anxious and I am not stressed when I have my poodle.

At my office, there are usually just as many personal pets as there are patients. We all take our dogs to work and many of us have more than one dog. Some of my employees even bring their cats. We have long shifts and our days with our pets are so few, and having a familiar, fluffy face at your job can make such a difference. If work is getting you down and you need some unbridled affection and comfort, you have your dog ready and willing to oblige. This rings true for all pet owners, but can be especially valuable for people on the autism spectrum.

My youngest stepdaughter is in law school and works at a law office during the summer. She is allowed to bring her dog to work with her. She does not have autism; she is actually highly social and outgoing, but she loves her dog and it brings her comfort to have her near. Many businesses and companies are recognizing the human-animal bond and allowing it to flourish in the workplace. Her dog is about twenty pounds and still portable. Her dog can sleep unobtrusively under her desk and is friendly to others. A dog of this size is easy to transport and integrates well into an office setting. The dog has limited training but she is affectionate and social, which puts her in the good graces of others.

The unsocialized dog may not be welcome at school or other public events, but it doesn't make him a bad dog. Just as autism has a spectrum of abilities and limitations, so does the dog. At home, he can be a guardian with limited outings. I would never directly advocate for a dog that bites, though I do have one that does. My husband is a police officer and, as an emergency veterinarian, I see injured police dogs often in addition to simply mean dogs. There is a place for dogs to bite, and they should be carefully trained to their task and managed by their owners when needed. Police dogs come in muzzled and will lay still when their handler requests them to do so, allowing a thorough exam. They have even been hospitalized for days, allowing treatments and handling by various staff members. Their bite has a place, and they know their job. They are trained to allow handling when necessary.

Mean dogs are much more difficult to treat. Their bite does not have a place or a reason. They are usually just afraid and lack good training experiences. Often, their owners are afraid of them too, so they cannot put a muzzle on them without getting bitten. These dogs have to be sedated for exam and treatment, which can make them more afraid and panicked during their stay and, possibly, the next visit. A little proper training could go a long way.

Not all mean dogs were "born that way" and I would dare to say that very few, if any, actually are. Personalities can be abrupt, like grumpy people, or even fearful and shy, but intent to harm is very different. It is usually a dog that has not been properly socialized or properly handled. Most of the time, he has just been left to his own devices, chained for long periods, or lacks in general interaction. This dog doesn't have to have been beaten or mistreated (though that is also a very real factor), he may simply be just neglected and frustrated. He could have been bred to guard or chase and has no outlet for his inner drives. Without proper interactions, he can become anxious, confused, and hyperactive. He can respond to uncertain situations with extreme defensiveness and bite when approached, restrained, or accidentally harmed simply because he doesn't know any better. This is how children get bitten in their own home by their own dog. There is no fault except for lack of training. The dog doesn't know how to respond appropriately when presented with a novel circumstance and thus gravitates to aggression and defensiveness very quickly. He lacks confidence and patience perhaps because he has never been exposed to those important concepts. The dog may be very reluctant to leave his personal space and very protective when it is breached. Mean dogs can and will bite anyone for the smallest offense or infringement; they think only of themselves and are not willing to engage in outside activities. This is not the same as a guard dog. A guard dog has confidence, he knows who belongs and who doesn't and dares not bear his teeth to his family. He may be aggressive to strangers, but it is only protection, not aggression. He engages readily with his family and will allow handling without fear. He doesn't have to be a mean dog to be an excellent guard dog or protector.

There is a distinct difference. If your dog bites protecting its home, it can be considered normal behavior and trustworthy as long as it is able to turn off the aggression when the owner asks. My dog, Grace, will allow you into the home when the family is there, but not when we are gone. She allows handling and will lay quietly for exam and treatments. She may not allow an intruder into our home; therefore, her bite has a place, but she can be restrained without risk to herself or others. Your dog may protect its home and property and still be well behaved at the veterinary office and tolerant to exam.

Small dogs can be aggressive, too, but nobody really talks about it because they rarely inflict wounds. The Chihuahua, for instance, has the greatest number of biters in their population, but it's generally nothing worth going to the human hospital for treatment. This kind of attitude may not be appropriate for a child with autism who is learning personal boundaries and space limitations. An older child might have better luck with such a beast or consider better training on behalf of the dog.

A dog of any breed will be devoted to its family and be the absolute best at its job. And if you really want an Irish wolfhound, by all means, get one. Do your research and be prepared to provide the intellectual and physical interaction the dog requires to be a well-behaved member of the household so neither of you regret the decision. Collie, spaniel, poodle, mutt, or Xoloitzcuintli can all be good choices with proper training and preparedness. There are 340 recognized dog breeds in the world. Surely, you can find a perfect size and type for your home. Each has its own unique quality, personality, and designated traits. All are wonderful and perfect for their purpose. They could be perfect in your home, perfect for your child. A dog's virtues are so valuable, be prepared to be amazed!

Chapter 4

The
"Pet Effect"
is Real

There is a saying about the closeness that certain people share, which makes them "family" and not just friends. They are people who are not genetically related but are highly emotionally bonded. This phenomenon extends to dogs as well. Dogs are much more attuned and connected to people than even other people can be. Sharing a household may help you to understand the habits of others, but it doesn't prepare you to bond with them, regardless of the relationship. Dogs are family, and yet so much more. Many individuals refer to their pet as their "fur baby," "little girl," or state they "love her like a child." I think dogs reciprocate this love. Their only source of connection is their people. They don't leave the house to visit friends or go to work. Their time is 100 percent focused on their owner(s) and their home. They are highly bonded, whether the person acknowledges it or not.

Dogs thrive on a conversation they don't need to reply to; they just listen. You could accidentally step on their tail or trip over them and their forgiveness is instant and sincere. Nowhere will you ever find such devotion to your cause or such love and genuineness.

The bond is strengthened by touch and play: things that are sometimes difficult for a person with autism to get "right" with a neurotypical person. Most people try to pat a dog. Dogs accept this, but do they like it? Do you want to be patted? As a person with autism, I touch my dog. I simply place my hand on her side. I feel her warmth. I enjoy her softness. I don't rub her. I don't pat her. I just touch her. This is our bond, our communication. She accepts it. My hand is extended in kindness, she revels in its simplicity.

I am married to a considerate person who has learned to tolerate the idiosyncrasies of autism. I hold his hand because I understand that to be the socially-accepted version of affection between married people. I much prefer to just be next to him, to sit quietly and look at the stars; to know he is near and to feel his warmth, to just be close. I learned this with my dogs as a child. We were physically close. We napped together in the sun and cuddled in the dark. I learned to be a good friend from an entirely different species: my dog. My affection with my childhood dogs promoted touch, and I learned not to fear it. I am not afraid or anxious. My dogs have taught me that touch is okay, that the positive outcomes overwhelm the negative.

Owning a dog comes with a high degree of physical interaction, instigated or not. Their coat needs regular bathing and occasional grooming. They may jump onto you when you get home in leaps of joy and lick your hand. The dog will brush against you in play and lean in for affection, lay quietly at your side to nap, even touch you just to assure you that they are there. It can be ignored or trained away, or it can be cherished and adopted.

A child could learn that brief physical encounters are safe and sometimes welcome. Dogs don't have to hold hands, but they can learn to shake. They don't know how to hug, but they can be a soft shoulder to embrace. Rubbing and petting can be therapy for both. It strengthens the bond and builds trust and communication. Affection is amazing whether it is given or received, it does wonders for the souls of both. How pleasing to give happiness in a touch, to receive love in a gesture. Two entirely different species are able to express a common emotion, with no uncertain interpretation, no unclear directive. It's just kindness. Love. Acceptance.

Dogs can teach children about taking turns and sharing. They don't reprimand when it is not done properly and are ever eager for their turn. Their gratefulness for a shared snack or a tossed frisbee is impossible to miss. He easily encourages more incidents and a willingness to participate. This type of exercise is a form of social bonding. Your child could learn how to interact with peers through his or her interactions with your dog. At the very least, your child will smile and laugh—the universal language of joy.

Your dog's adoring affection is also therapy. You have distractions: your phone, your spouse or family, your work or habits outside the home. There are things pulling you away from your dog at all times, things that you may prioritize periodically and that occasionally have much more pressing needs. That will never happen with the dog's attention. The members of his household are his only charge. He will never be too busy or distracted to pay attention. He won't cringe at the thought of playing ball again, the thirty-seventh time today. He doesn't care whose turn it is. He happily provides instant attention and inter-

action. He will make you feel important and like your time is valued. His devotion will give you and your child confidence. It could be the psychological support needed to encourage your child to go to the park or street fair. It may perpetuate more extroverted behaviors and social engagement.

My childhood dogs provided the positive interactions I needed to become successful in the human world. I was able to practice talking with them. I became habituated to touch and I learned to play. There is nothing more freeing than laughter, especially laughter originated by play.

Dogs are quick to play: they spontaneously chase their tail, they fetch toys. My dog takes a ball to the couch and drops it off the other side, then zips around to find where it went, only to do it all over again. Dogs invite you to play, too. They bring you the ball, the toy, or a happy waggle, begging to be chased. They are silly and unaffected by judgment or socially-dictated "acceptable" behaviors. They don't care what you think. They don't care if you are busy or tired or grumpy. They will play at any time, for any reason. They don't have formal games that require rules or traditional protocols. You can respond any way you choose. They get funnier with engagement and laughter. They respond well to whatever you have to offer. Dogs promote engagement that leads to touch and laughter and so much well-being that one can't help but feel content. They're an instant antidepressant.

Laughter is a universal human language. Babies learn to laugh before they talk. It is the easiest expression of joy a person makes without words. It can eventually stimulate talk. Dogs bring out laughter with their normal behavior, it doesn't even require training. Even now, as an adult, I chase my dog around the couch or the island when she grabs a toy and runs. She encourages me to laugh. One is never too old to enjoy the little things. A little exercise releases endorphins and makes one healthier. Laughter is healthy, freeing, and it builds confidence. How can you be hesitant and laugh at the same time? It's dogs' gift to the world: to lift our spirits like only a best friend can do.

The pet effect is real. There are scientists, veterinarians, and researchers trying to understand the miracles of pet ownership. They have recognized the impact of the human-animal bond on mental health and wellbeing and are attempting to rationalize it. Lots of luck to them. There are wondrous things in this universe that we shall never explain, and the canine is one of them. What other animal is completely dependent on us for survival and is grateful?

The cat can be feral and hunt to survive. Given a loving home, the cat returns affection but still lives independently, choosing to wander the neighborhood if given a chance and sometimes not returning for days. The chicken can free range to some degree but has no presence of mind to avoid dangers and would easily succumb to predators. A chicken can't be housebroken or respect your space, it

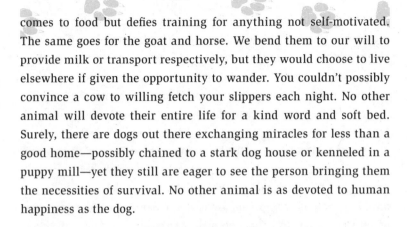

comes to food but defies training for anything not self-motivated. The same goes for the goat and horse. We bend them to our will to provide milk or transport respectively, but they would choose to live elsewhere if given the opportunity to wander. You couldn't possibly convince a cow to willing fetch your slippers each night. No other animal will devote their entire life for a kind word and soft bed. Surely, there are dogs out there exchanging miracles for less than a good home—possibly chained to a stark dog house or kenneled in a puppy mill—yet they still are eager to see the person bringing them the necessities of survival. No other animal is as devoted to human happiness as the dog.

Humans Could Learn Much from Dogs

Humans are not as good to each other as dogs are to us. We have failed at universally accepting others, those who are different or unfamiliar. We are judgmental. We have rules and we rarely instigate spontaneous play. Our sole purpose is not to make others happy, but to satisfy ourselves. We could learn a lot from dogs. We could bring out the best in each other to foster respect and kindness. We could deserve the loyalty that dogs give us. The saying "be the person your dog thinks you are" has serious merit. Your dog thinks you are the best being on the planet and the only one capable of providing them with life-giving affection and attention. You could not feed them for twenty-four hours and they would still be happy to see you, even if you arrived with no food. They would choose you empty handed over the stranger with food. How do we deserve that? Kindness. Forgiveness. Acceptance. You have so much to learn and gain from a dog.

Many people believe a child will acquire responsibility with pet ownership. That your child could learn to be dependable and accountable while broadening their social horizons sounds simply amazing, and it is quite possibly true. Caring for another life is nurturing and empowering. It gives a sense of independence that perpetuates self-discovery. My early exposures to animals gave me confidence in my ability to heal and provide. The dog has routine and consistency, which many crave. Most importantly, he provides rewards; he is always happy to see you, responds well to kindness, and doesn't care if you talk or are quiet. He doesn't mind if you are clumsy or slow. Whatever you have to offer, dogs accept and are grateful. Same dinner as yesterday, great! Got fed last this time, oh well! You're an hour late, still happy to see you! Absent is the criticism that humans are quick to toss with careless abandon at the slightest of perceived offense. Animals don't scold you for being less than perfect. They are never trite over your deficiencies. On no occasion is a harsh word (or bark) spoken in your direction for trivial matters.

If you have more than one dog, you learn the alpha dog is not mean. She doesn't bite or growl at others. When she wants something, she approaches and waits for them to notice and concede. She just asks, and they listen. We could learn a lot from their example.

We don't have to berate others or tear them down to be the boss. We don't have to be greater in stature to be first. We don't have to be domineering to be right. We could just ask, extend an olive branch, and hope not to get pruned. If only all of our human social interactions were as simple as those exhibited by dogs!

Dog Hierarchy

Do you know what the dog's social hierarchy consists of? Not the biggest in the group. It's the oldest and/or most confident dog in the pack. I have a four-pound toy poodle and three other dogs that weigh over forty pounds each, but the tiniest dog rules them all! Leadership is gained by commanding allegiance, not invoking fear. Tiny Bazinga is the leader of her pack. She is younger than the hunting dogs and the same age as the standard poodle, but she is more confident. She is bold and outgoing, where the standard is shy and hesitant. Bazinga eats first, she gets first choice of new toys, and she gets her favorite spot on the couch, even forcing others to move if she chooses. She is not mean. She doesn't bite them. She doesn't growl at them. She is just sure of herself and kind. I observe my dogs and learn—my best friends will never lead me astray.

Chapter 5

Do You Need a Service Dog? Emotional Support Dog? Therapy Dog?

P et ownership is a privilege and comes with great responsibility. It is an investment of time and money. Dogs have
needs and we are morally (and legally, to some degree)
obliged to fulfill their demands.

Pet ownership comes with a duty to properly train
and socialize the pet to avoid noise complaints, destructive behavior, and potential accidents (like escaping, fear biting, and separation
anxiety). You also have to clean up after them and exercise them regu-
larly. Vaccinations and licensing may be required in your community,
and deworming benefits everyone exposed to your backyard. Aside
from the normal welfare requirements of living beings (food, water,
and shelter), dogs also need companionship. They thrive with interaction, as do people. Consistent interaction is training, because it's
conditioning the pet to handling and experiences.

If you can afford it and feel it is warranted, you can send your dog to a trainer. There are obedience classes, agility sports, and guarding courses available for all breeds of dogs. The question remains, is it necessary? The house dog really has one job and only one job: companionship. No training required.

Good behavior is a must, but not expensive schooling. There are fabulous, well-trained, and expensive therapy and service dogs available, but they won't bring any more to your life or your child's development than a household pet. They may be a loyal companion and rescue their owner from whatever circumstance they are trained to, but they are still a family dog. Even with fancy training and important titles, he is still a pet. You will not be able to look at an intensively trained animal and differentiate it from any other pet. He or she will bond to their family as much as they are capable to with no regard to training. It has to be a genuine service animal to be accepted in more public places, but even that is highly variable. A lesson in nomenclature may help to understand this conundrum.

A service animal is recognized by the Americans with Disabilities Act of 1990 (ADA) as an animal that has been individually trained to perform tasks for people with disabilities, such as guiding people who are blind, alerting people who are deaf, pulling wheelchairs, alerting and protecting a person who has seizures, or performing other special tasks. They are to help with a specific impairment that limits one or more life activities due to a physical or mental disability. Service animals are working animals, not pets. There are laws protecting their status so that they can escort their people into public spaces normally exclusionary to animals. Service animals are socially well behaved and are neither outgoing nor fearful; they are focused on their job. They should not be engaged with petting or feeding, since they are working whenever they are with their person.

Service animals are allowed into restaurants, and since they are well behaved they usually lay down and wait for their owner. They do not beg for food and they ignore other patrons. A restaurant owner may not challenge the person's disability, but they can ask if the dog is trained to perform a certain task and what that task is, which, in a sense, describes the disability. The response "he helps me calm down" is not acceptable. The dog has to be trained to a specific task recognized by the Americans with Disabilities Act or it is not a true service animal. The task can be simple; for example, the Great Dane

that braces for his owner when he is unsteady on his feet, like a walking crutch, or the peanut alert dog that may save its owner's life by circumventing exposure.

Service Animals can be very expensive, especially those assisting the blind. They are trained for years and are highly intelligent. Their person's life may be dependent upon their skills, and they have to be 100 percent trustworthy at all times. A service animal has a very serious job and is not to be taken lightly. Service animals do exist for those on the autism spectrum when the degree of impairment qualifies as a disability. Those dogs have been carefully selected and conditioned to accept severely polar emotional outbursts and overwhelming anxiety that can cripple their person. They are trained to be very tolerant and steady in the face of unpredictable reactions that interfere with daily life.

The jacket a service dog wears does not qualify it for the job. Those vests can be ordered online for any dog of indeterminate size and disposition, no doubt lacking the credentials to warrant it. I've seen snarling Chihuahuas with those jackets—since when is a Chihuahua capable of performing the duties of a golden retriever as a service animal? What, exactly, could it be trained to do that would mitigate a disability recognized by the ADA?

For most of us on the spectrum, we don't experience limits in life's activities, it's the social spectrum where we struggle. If anything, we would qualify for an emotional support animal.

An emotional support animal is not granted as many special privileges by law, though that may be changing. To qualify for an emotional support animal, a physician must recognize and diagnose a psychological condition, such as post-traumatic stress disorder or another anxiety disorder, and prescribe a pet companion for emotional support. Physicians have long recognized that pet companionship has unprecedented benefits for those suffering from anxiety, bipolar syndrome, depression, and occasional suicidal thoughts. They concede that a person is not alone if they have a pet and, therefore, they will have fewer distressing episodes and thoughts while caring for their pet. By actually prescribing a companion, physicians ensure that its benefits are truly taken seriously. That companion is usually a dog, but it can be a cat or other household pet. It is usually a pet the person already has, or intends to acquire, and it is not specifically trained. The prescription is designed to allow the pet access to otherwise restricted areas, such as housing with a no-pet policy or flying as a regular passenger on a plane instead of cargo. The title "emotional support animal" has no implication in its training, behavior, or social adaptiveness. Unlike a service animal, it does not meet rigorous standards of training and is not always an intelligent specimen. It is simply a pet that provides comfort and companionship. It is no different than any other pet on the planet, except that it has a prescription from a physician allowing it to be housed in buildings typically denied to pets.

An emotional support animal is not allowed into restaurants or other public places. Its title does not grant it access to privileges reserved for service animals, such as staying in hotels or going into grocery stores. It may help its owner struggle through a panic attack by providing a warm and loving presence, and it may give comfort in stressful environments by being a loyal friend, but it is not specifically trained to mitigate a problem.

Many people falsely state that their emotional support animal is a service animal. The mistake is usually innocent, but the verbiage is important. The emotional support animal provides a service to them, but it is not the ADA-recognized service animal that defies restrictions. The emotional support animal is still just a pet. Service animals have earned their right to be in public places, like a store or restaurant, but it is possible household pets are ruining it for service dogs because the emotional support animal doesn't have the same training and/or specific duties that service dogs have. Restaurants and grocery stores need to keep a level of hygiene and require a modicum of composure on the part of an animal.

Most emotional support animals lack the proper training to be allowed into public places. Remember, there are no official guidelines for qualification and no formalized training for their jobs. They are just pets, and most pets aren't exposed routinely to large crowds enough to be okay with it. They can be aggressive, loud, or cause havoc. They just aren't well adapted or socialized to focus on their one true purpose: companionship to their person. Housepets are easily distracted by others and are often overwhelmed by large public gatherings.

When people see an animal that pulls at their leash, barks, or otherwise misbehaves, they recognize that it definitely isn't a real service animal—which sometimes holds consequences for genuine service animals. It can lead business owners to be more confrontational when a service animal is attempting to frequent their establishment or put pressure on a person who has a service animal to prove  they're legitimate. The emotional support animal has a high probability of creating a bad impression of those with service animals that really need to be there.

Emotional support animals absolutely have value. The title has a purpose, particularly because canine companionship really does have true therapeutic benefits. If someone is going to try to exploit the system, he should at least train his dog so it is socially acceptable. The pet should be disciplined enough to lay quietly for a few hours on a plane so everyone can get through the tedious ordeal of flying. Good behavior will foster less stress and anxiety for the pet as well as his flight companion. You may also be allowed to have your household pet travel to school or work. If you have a prescription and your dog is well behaved, he may be granted access when he is needed the most, in social settings. The law does not require schools to recognize emotional support animals, but many voluntarily choose to allow them. Having a well-behaved, leash-trained, and moderately obedient dog will further ensure his admittance.

The dog that is typically allowed into schools is the therapy dog. Like service animals, therapy animals have endured vigorous training with high standards of achievement and adhere to strict rules and laws to gain their title. They have good, basic obedience skills that have been tested and certified. Contrasting them to service animals that attend a single person, therapy animals have a special aptitude to work with the public. They interact with many people, not just one-on-one. There is a registry for therapy animals, and they have a specific handler. The handler ensures the safety of the dog and those that interact with it (discouraging ear-pulling and reducing the incident of petting too hard). They lack ADA access like a service animal but are treated as more than just pets.

Therapy animals serve their community through animal-assisted interventions: activities, education, and visits. They can be found volunteering at retirement homes, hospitals, and airports to reduce stress and provide a social lubricant. Their job, though brief, is connecting with those in emotionally trying or physically distressing situations. Their presence at Alzheimer's facilities and hospice centers has well-documented benefits and purpose. For that reason, they are allowed access to areas where most pets are constrained. However, their access is limited to time with their handler. You could own a therapy dog, but he would not automatically be allowed to attend school with you or your child with autism. A therapy animal is for the benefit of the public when it is with its designated handler in a public setting. Any other time, under control of any other person, the dog is just a pet. The therapy animal could service the classroom as a group, including your child, but it would not be realigned to service only to your child under its title of therapy animal.

A person wanting to help those on the autism spectrum could invest their time and funds into a therapy animal, which could perpetuate ownership of a dog in the future by providing positive exposures. Brief interactions may lay a foundation that a family lacking a dog could build upon. Many children, especially children with autism, can be easily overwhelmed by bouncing rambunctious puppies, but they can willingly engage with a stoic and patient therapy dog. I can't express enough the importance of a well-trained dog.

You don't need to buy or train a service or therapy dog to have profound improvements in your child's development. You don't even need a prescription for an emotional support animal. Those are just labels, which neither the dog nor your child understands. You simply need to go down to the local shelter and pick out a friend. You can call it a guide dog if you want, because it will be giving some direction in life. The dog will no doubt be supportive and protective of its charge, so it can be an emotional support animal. It will serve you well, so it is a service animal, but, mostly, it is just your pet that loves its family and will be there for whatever task of companionship he or she is challenged to fulfill.

If you have the necessary funds to spend on a service dog and feel that your child needs one, by all means, invest in one. If a prescription for an emotional support animal will increase the odds of bringing the pet to social events, get one. Otherwise, just get a dog and train it well so that it can enhance experiences and bring joy to your household.

As a veterinarian, I cannot tell the difference between a service animal, emotional support animal, therapy animal, and general household pet if it is obedient and well socialized. In contrast, I can absolutely tell which dog is not a service animal or therapy animal based solely on its bad behavior. So, get a good dog and treat it well. Explore the miraculous power of pet ownership, because no label is required.

Chapter 6

Basic Concepts:
Training Your Dog

I was raised without television. I didn't attend the movies until I was a married adult. Because of that, I missed all the inaccurate portrayals of dog ownership over which Hollywood has entire generations of dog lovers swooning. I had to devise my own ideas of canine behavior. I had no idea collies would spontaneously go for help should one fall down a well. Little did I know that German shepherds could problem solve or a scruffy terrier dog could reason and intervene in complex human problems. If I had been raised with knowledge of all that glorious potential, my poor dog would have been trained to oblivion.

Luckily for all my childhood pets, they were required to master only basic obedience skills and a few random parlor tricks. Their job was not to save the world from outlandish hypothetical scenarios. Their job was to be there for me, to be the one accepting soul that never compromised my feelings or expectations. My dog was my quiet therapy in a complex world which could not be tamed.

You can expect a lot out of your dog, and I hope he or she can comply. Remember that just as autism has a spectrum, so does the canine have the capacity to learn. Certain breeds are more willing to learn, and individual dogs within breeds are more intelligent and obliging than their peers. Your household is unique and your dog's position in the home is equally distinct. Any breed and any dog can be trained to do just about

anything, some are just better at certain things. You can choose a dog based on any number of traits, even if it's a sporting breed and you live in a subdivision. Just because you own a German shorthair pointer doesn't mean you have to be out hunting pheasants and grouse every weekend. You don't even have to be a sportsman. You just have to provide your dog with an outlet for its inherent drive to search and point.

The dog's job is first to be a companion to your child, but it may have more energy than can be extinguished reasonably with normal interactions, so be prepared to provide a channel appropriate to its needs or get a less-active breed of dog.

Burn Off Steam for Hyper Dogs

A good way to burn off steam is to play games of fetch. Rarely does it have to be trained into them, since most dogs will chase; some are more reluctant to return, however. For those that only chase, a storehouse of balls or frisbees will usually help. Throw them one at a time, and, after the dog has caught one and "conquered" the event, throw another one. Most of the time, they drop one and chase after the next. Once all the toys are at one end of the yard, walk down there and throw them back in the same order. Dogs with good recall may gradually adapt to returning the toy, but it may be work instead of play for some period of time before they get it right. Fetch is also a good way for children to interact with pets, since physical activity is important. My toy poodle rarely returns when games of fetch are attempted, but she gladly engages in games of "chase whoever has the toy" with her dog housemates and any person willing to give it a try. Children love this game, since she chases after them with gusto and will only run fast enough to keep ahead of them when it is her turn. She adapts her speed and enthusiasm to the situation, and I think this is true with most dogs. They love to play and will tailor the game to fit the players. Play with a dog will not lead to adverse experiences, like admonishment for not playing the game right, whose turn it is, or not sharing properly, because dogs don't care. They are just happy for the experience. Psychologists have long advocated for play in early childhood development to enhance learning and prepare for social interactions. It fosters connections, cooperation, and development of the imagination. Play is an important part of childhood. Your dog can encourage its manifestation. It's hard to say "no" to a wagging tail and bouncing ball.

Play

Certain types of play can be trained into your dog, like hide and seek. Start by hiding the toy in the next room and escorting them to find it with words to encourage them. I ask my poodle, "Where is your bunny?" (her preferred stuffed toy), which she readily searches for when I ask. She has many toys, but her bunny is the favorite. She is very smart, and if the bunny ever accidentally permanently disappears, I'll no doubt have to find one very similar to replace it or risk looking ridiculous calling her stuffed chicken a bunny. I'm sure she doesn't know the difference from a bunny or chicken, except that one is her favorite. None of my other dogs have favorite toys. I wish I could say that she is an anomaly, but dogs are individuals.

Play can also be training if your dog is highly motivated. I had a Labrador retriever that would learn just about anything for a kind word. She responded to hand signals and knew many parlor tricks. She accepted learning as a game, and when she got it right, she was noticeably happy about it. I felt I really communicated with her and she truly understood me. I felt a tremendous amount of trust and contentment with her while playing with her. She was the smartest dog I have ever known.

When people talk about bringing a person with autism "outside of their shell," I think this may be what they're referring to. My Labrador was able

to respond easily to nonverbal cues and I learned to communicate without words. I didn't have to talk, and she responded. I blossomed with the ability to make a connection. I gained confidence and transitioned in getting involved in human interactions.

Learning and training are lifetime events for people and their pets. After the basic commands are grasped by our dogs, we usually forget to continue the learning process. That's okay. A well-behaved dog is usually one that has mastered "come," "sit," the leash, is crate trained, and has polite manners (like "don't jump on people" or "no stealing food from the counters"). To train your dog to these things, it just takes a little time and persistence.

The Leash

The leash is the best place to start, since it gives you absolute control of the dog—and he should respect that. Dogs that pull at the leash should be pulled back as a quick reminder that you are in charge. Absolutely do not go and buy a harness! No harnesses! If they pull, you pull. Don't give them leverage and the ability to put their entire weight into the end of the leash! That will not prevent them from pulling, it will give them the ability to pull harder. Small dogs with tracheal problems should be handled in harnesses, but not huskies, who were bred for centuries to commandeer sleds.

The leash also gives you an opportunity to discipline behavior like jumping onto people (a gentle pull to unbalance the dog usually does the trick), which will quickly restore their attention to you where it belongs. Most dogs love the leash and overlook the few times it is used to discipline them. Getting the leash out should mean good things: a walk, exercise, and time with you. It could also mean the dog will stay with you or your child, regardless of the distractions. It can keep them safe in traffic and prevent an accident.

The Crate

The crate should also mean good things. Your dog should have a safe spot, a place that only he or she visits and is free from the other members of the household. This is their personal crate. The crate is not punishment and not a place to be feared. All my dogs have their own crates and they love them, most of them sleep in their crates of their own free will. When they have a bone or other treat, they usually zip to their crate where they know no one will steal it from them or harass them. When we have company over, my standard poodle is overwhelmed and goes to her crate to avoid inter- action. A crate is a quiet place

with her own bed and toys, which are reserved only for her. Rarely do I lock my dogs in their crates, except when they were puppies and being housebroken. A crate is a safe place your dog can escape to when needed that teaches them confinement is not castigation.

If your dog ever needs to be boarded or hospitalized for any reason, crate training will make that event a much less stressful one. I have seen dogs that panic when confined, and they usually spend their time in the veterinary hospital heavily sedated. It makes it very difficult to assess treatment progress and overall health if the dog cannot be confined for a short period of time. You will be doing your pet a favor by encouraging it to accept short periods in a crate.

Basic Commands

Other things that make life a little safer are basic obedience commands: "come" and "sit." Good recall could save your dog's life if, for example, he had an opportunity to run into the street but immediately returns when called. It also allows your dog time off the leash outside of the yard (like when hiking or in parks) because you know he will return to you on demand. Good recall is difficult to establish in certain breeds, like Anatolian shepherds, Saint Bernards, Jack Russel terriers, and all manner of hounds, amongst others. It can be done with many sessions on a long line that forces return when called every time, until the dog thinks there is no alternative. There are dogs that may forget or get distracted and become reluctant to return. Never disciple a slow return because that will make them less likely to return next time— every return is a good one. Be consistent and remember that it may be a lifelong process with some dogs. If you have already made a lifetime commitment to be consistent and patient with your child, remember that a dog is a member of your household and deserves the same.

Trainers

There are trainers that advocate for rewards or treats to modify behavior, but what happens when you can't pay the dog for good services? Or worse, what if your dog is a resource guarder? These dogs aren't aggressive, they are just worried about losing what they have. This sometimes manifests in dogs that have gone hungry or lacked proper interactions and toys. Any opportunity to have food or toys (resources), they will protect with enthusiasm. Trying to train them with a

piece of food may actually be distracting, because all they can think about is gaining and keeping the food. Some of these dogs snap quickly to gain the food and will snap or growl to keep the food. This is not positive training. This is dangerous. There are methods to overcome much of this behavior, and I would strongly recommend them to avoid an accident. Treat training should be reserved for the dog that takes food kindly and safely while not obsessing about it.

The dog should be willing to learn, and not only for food. Praise and affection should also motivate your friend. It is true that the most easily trained dogs are treat-motivated, but the most intelligent dogs are self-motivated. At some point in your lifetime, you should witness a herding animal at work, even if it is only on video. The farmer tells the border collie or Australian cattle dog to bring the sheep into a specific gate, and she does. No treat. No direction. No verbal cues. No hand signals. She was told what to do and she figures it out. That dog is not treat-motivated; she is goal-motivated. She knows what needs to be done and makes it happen. She moves thirty to forty sheep at a time, not missing one, and gets them all through the proper gate safely. The farmer's expectations of her ability and the dog's capacity to perform align perfectly. Hidden are the months and years of training and the dog's natural instincts to herd and respond. Notice it is not a papillon or a poodle out there making it happen, it's a dog naturally suited to the job.

I am sure there are non-herding dogs that can be trained to herd, as there are all manner of possibilities for the right dog molded in the skillful hands of a dedicated trainer. The key to proper dog training is patience. Autism isn't about limitations; it's about understanding and proper direction, and so is training a dog. Dogs need kind guidance and proper instructions to learn. Some will not be master more than a few commands and a wagging tail. Some will make Lassie envious. Your dog just needs to be a good citizen, so she is welcome in your home and can work her magic. How she performs at agility trials and sporting events are secondary to her true value of companionship. Parlor tricks are just showing off, and while there are those that really excel at them, your dog's manners are your preference and her tricks your prerogative. Reward her with whatever works: treats, belly rubs, toys, praise. Whatever makes her day, make it wonderful. She will, in turn, make your day wonderful.

Vet Care

Occasionally, your pet may need to visit the veterinarian for routine care. This is where I would like to make the most impression. Your dog can be whatever it wants in your home as long as you tolerate it, but at the veterinary clinic, he needs to be a good citizen. Please practice good discipline. The veterinarian needs to examine the dog, touch it, and vaccinate it. To accommodate this, your dog should walk willingly on a leash, sit patiently when instructed to do so, and not panic when approached by a stranger. Your dog's confidence in your leadership will often dictate his response to new stimuli.

If you have never provided your dog direction, he will not be willing to endure new experiences without fear. He will not be able to trust you to get him through it. Just as you expect the dog to willingly support you or your child by his presence and calming attitude, you need to provide the dog that support while at the veterinary office. This will make the entire process easier for everybody. Even the nicest dogs may bite when they are scared and cornered. Don't program them to act irrationally because you didn't give them confidence while handling them at the vet.

Some people claim their dog doesn't like veterinarians. Really? We certainly don't all look alike, so how does your dog know I'm a veterinarian? Are dogs anxious to cross my lawn because a veterinarian lives at that home? While out walking my own dog, do they run the other way because a veterinarian is on the loose? No. Dogs don't fear the veterinarians, they don't know the difference between me and anybody else. Dogs fear the unknown. Dogs also fear what have been, in the past, painful experiences. Brief, positive experiences can extinguish fear.

If I got vaccinated every time I went to the doctor, I would also hate going, so take the dog for a weight check or stop in for a cookie. Veterinarians encourage this training! They want good experiences, too. Don't make every episode at the veterinary office a dreaded fiasco for you and your dog. Your dog reads you. He gets cues from you. If you are upset, there must be something amiss, so try to be as patient as you expect him to be. Remember his only exposure to the world is through you, so make it pleasant.

Don't take him into the vet to get his nails clipped because you think you can't do it at home. Learn to do it. Your dog trusts you; you are the leading expert on his tolerances, preferences, and idiosyncrasies. If he doesn't like his nails trimmed, trim one nail a day followed by his favorite thing. Soon, he will tolerate nail clipping because he trusts you. He's never going to trust the veterinarian because we are going to have to have a staff member hold him down, muzzle him, and forcibly trim every nail before returning him to you with no reward. He's going to hate the vet more every time he visits! You can make it a positive experience because you know him. You can trim one nail a day for sixteen days to make a pleasant experience out of it. You feed him every day. Trim one nail before breakfast every day or just pretend to clip a few nails, then reward him. He will soon get the picture.

Biting dogs are an exception to this method. If your dog will actually bite you, then you need more focused training on general behavior (and not the nails). Your dog doesn't respect you and is dangerous if he bites. Should you intend to keep such a dog in your home, precautions need to be made so that the dog doesn't bite when accidentally cornered or vexed. Anybody could make a mistake and cross the tolerance threshold with this type of dog at any time, so please don't put an innocent person in danger. Mostly, these dogs lack confidence. They can be trained; however, for a home with children, it is not a safe combination.

It's Okay to Admit Defeat

There are myriads of friendly dogs needing homes, so there's no reason to put anybody in jeopardy when safe options exist. Training a dog is a talent, and not everyone has it. It is okay to admit defeat and either send the dog to a trainer or re-home it. The basic obedience concepts can be mastered by anyone with a dog, leash, and a crate, but complex behavior modifications should be left to the experts. You have enough on your plate.  You don't need to make adding a dog an exercise in exacerbation. The dog is supposed to help you with his own version of animal therapy; it should not require therapy of its own.

Basic Training Shouldn't Be Difficult

The idea of training your dog should not be frightening. Your daily interactions with him will train him. You get up, you let him out of his crate and take the dog outside to potty. You say his name and feed him. He learns to sleep in the crate, go outside, and he comes to his name in just a few days because he has engaged in consistently repeated and rewarded activities. A few walks on the leash and he's a stellar citizen. Just as these few things habituate your dog to his expected responsibilities in your home, a few exposures to a child with autism will habituate the dog to that interaction. If your child is non-verbal and subject to random vocal outbursts to express emotions, the dog will learn to accept them. Your dog doesn't speak English (or French, for that matter)—he doesn't know if your child is articulate or not. He can sense emotion, though. He can be comforting and patient when your child is upset or silly and playful when your child is happy. He doesn't know the words; he reads the emotions. He can learn to reciprocate within the environment he is exposed to: kindness and patience. He can be steadfast during meltdowns and accepting of outbursts. He doesn't have to know what yelling is, because it could be happy or exacerbated, yet he will respond with gentleness. This is the only home he knows, and this will be normal to him. Your dog can provide all the wonderous acceptance you are hoping for your child, with no expensive training required. Just let them be together. Let them get to know and be there for each other.

My personal dog was not raised with children, yet she is very excited to engage with them. She is tender and careful not to scare them or take a toy too quickly. She allows them to hold her, though they lack the skills to do so properly (by the neck at times) and does

not wiggle or bite. She was never trained to be still while they struggle to pick her up. She is just patient, because she was taught patience and she extrapolated that to all things. I revel in consistency and my dog has blossomed as a result. She is social and engaging, though I did not teach her those things directly. I taught her to trust and be kind. Your dog is capable of great things if you can offer him kindness and trust. You will appear to be an expert trainer by your willingness to be patient. If you give to your dog what you expect for him to give back, you will not be disappointed.

Chapter 7

Dogs are Heroes

A quick online search will find you thousands if not millions of true stories about dog heroism: dogs that alerted their owners because of a fire in the home, dogs who have warded off intruders, and dogs who have physically placed themselves in harm's way to save their person by defending against cougars and bears.

Some dogs have rescued children from drowning, kept them warm and safe overnight when they wandered lost into the woods, and sought help when needed. Dogs are smarter than most people give them credit and more passionate about their humans than we realize. They would absolutely die for us. They consider not their size and strength against grizzly bears or mountain lions; they would die trying to protect their person, with no thought to fear or reason. Those who criticize dogs as "lesser beings" because they're not capable of deductive reasoning should be challenged to explain these tales of heroism. They are the only heroes truly lacking selfish motives. Your dog doesn't have to save you from the jaws of death to be a hero; he can save you from yourself. His act of heroism is just as profound, just as marvelous. I have seen it.

Working at the emergency clinic, many clients feel compelled to explain why their dog is so important to them. Little do they know, I already am familiar with the construct. My dog is my entire world, too. I love their stories and will listen with respect and patience. Given a chance, every dog that visits our clinic could have a gallant story of salvation waiting to be told, like the golden retriever that saved his owner while out hiking in the canyons of Utah. A flash flood occurred from a brief summer rain, which was trapped in the narrow and beautiful ravine walls. His owner was enthralled with the deep grooves cut along the towering rocks, wondering how they could be formed when the very answer was about to roll down to them. His dog started barking and racing in circles, which was very out of character. Most likely, the dog could hear the water building momentum as the torrent was forcing itself through the slender gorge. When the owner approached his dog, the dog ran down the canyon. Luckily for them both, he followed. After a very short distance, he could hear the roar of the water as it spilled through the chasm and immediately recognized the danger. They ran to a place that had a shallow fork with rocks and ledges to climb upon. From the top of the chasm, they watched the dark and violent water spill past. His golden retriever had saved their lives.

Occasionally dogs do things that are intellectually calculating. They see danger and mitigate it, if at all possible. How do they recognize the threat? What makes them decide to resolve it in the way they do? One of my clients told me about his grandson wandering into the sorting corral, where they had cows in there milling around, calling for their recently weaned calves. The pen was small and held many cows with not much room to maneuver away from the rail. Their grandson was a toddler and did not understand the dangers of approaching the cows.

In a closely confined area, most cows are not looking where they are stepping, so they can easily trample anything under three feet tall. Their grandson had slipped under the rail and tottered into the pen. Their border collie zipped off from the porch and ran to his side. The dog was not raised with children, it was only trained to herd cattle. He was not told to go, and no one saw the problem until the dog took steps to alleviate it. The border collie ran to the pen and barked at the cows, placing himself between the child and the herd. He used his body to prevent the toddler from getting any closer to the cows and his herding instincts to keep the cows away. His actions drew the attention of his owners, so they were able to remove them both safely from the pen.

The dog's decision to place himself between the grandson and the cows was unprecedented bravery. He couldn't force the cows away from the child, since there was no room in the pen. He couldn't negotiate a way for the child out of the pen, since toddlers don't respond to herding. His choice to stand between the child and the danger and bark was judicious and valiant. It should be noted that most border collies don't bark when working, they are silent motivators. His actions seemed to be a cognitive decision based on the circumstances.

I met a tiny rat terrier who prevented his elderly owner from running into burglars. The woman had been out shopping in the late evening and had taken her rat terrier with her. When she returned to her home, the dog refused to go inside, barking and pacing instead. It took her several minutes to catch the dog, and he still remained apprehensive. His fear caused her to be more cautious when entering her home, where she found that it had been robbed.

While she was trying to understand her dog's reluctance to go inside, the burglars were going out the back door. Had she caught them in the act, she may have been harmed. One could say that fear motivated the rat terrier to resist entering its home, perhaps he knew he was unable to defend himself against the intruders, but his actions prevented an accident that could have had a terrible outcome.

I met a person who was actually robbed and physically assaulted. The person was reluctant to leave the house for weeks afterward. This interfered with work and daily living. A large dog was prescribed to help relieve her anxiety, and it completely transformed her life. The dog gave her confidence and a sense of protection, though he was not exactly trained for such. They ventured out on walks and joined activities that would not have been possible before, due to her crippling fear of the unknown.

Mental illness is just as life-threatening as physical illness and often not recognized or treated. Emotional support animals are prescribed when a physician has identified the problem. For many, that may come too late. Thankfully, dogs don't need a prescription to work their wonders, they just need to be invited into a home and become a

part of our lives. My older brother served in Afghanistan during the Iraq War as an Army soldier. He did not see very much conflict but spoke to many who had. After returning home, many of those soldiers were distant from the comradery that had bound them in a hostile country. My brother returned to his friends, family, and dogs. He adjusted well to civilian life and maintains a steady job and home.

Others have had a more difficult assimilation, especially those exposed to combat. Many of the veterans I have met have found solace in their dogs. Canine companionship is a return to the strong tie of having someone at your side every moment to protect and serve. They have found a partner who will not forsake them or let them down. Their dog's friendship keeps them grounded and provides a sense of self-worth. Many have told me that the only reason they haven't seriously contemplated suicide is because they are worried about leaving their dog behind.

Many veteran accounts of rehabilitation have their dogs at the core, including how they needed to be there for their pets for walks and activities. The passion in their voice for getting better is attributed to the love they have for their dog. Their dog is their comfort and a reason to get better, to become more mobile and active. The dog is the never-demanding physical therapist with a gentle motivation that cannot be ignored. I know of no person capable of resisting a wagging tail and deep, dark eyes.

Even those that say they don't want a dog may find they really do. As people get older, they worry that their pet may outlive them and are apprehensive about burdening their family. In my experience, I think the opposite occurs. Many times, at the emergency clinic, I am presented with a frail, old dog with heart failure and am told how important the dog is and how much they want to ensure its comfort, because it was their late grandma's dog and she loved it so. Never have I heard the opposite, where there was no commitment to care because the dog was not theirs at the beginning. They will do their best to assure grandma's dog is well cared for up to its very last days.

Occasionally, the emergency clinic is brought strays or dogs with unknown owners that have been injured. We do our best to reunite them with their family, but sometimes the family never comes forward. For those, I wonder if the owner has died, the pet has escaped the yard, and no one even knows to be looking for it. Some of these dogs end up at the local shelter, which will work diligently to find them a home. Those that require extensive care cannot be shifted to the pound, simply because they lack the funds and resources to care for them properly. At times, the emergency clinic will take them on as a personal mission of kindness. We fix them up at our own expense, donating our time and homes to rehabilitate them, and then rehome them at no charge. We cannot save them all, but occasionally we make a difference. We may have saved the life of the pet, but I know we have also enhanced the life of a new owner. There is just no denying the ripples that a caring act can produce.

Recently, the emergency clinic was presented a stray small terrier-type dog with a severe injury to a hind leg. No owner was to be found, even after days of searching. There was no saving the leg, but we felt compelled to save the dog. After a limb amputation and a short recovery period, the dog was due to be rehomed. A client heard his story and told us he had the perfect owner, "The most amazing match," as he put it. Only, that person wasn't actively looking for a dog. His plan was to take the dog to the person to see what happens.

Though risky (because he may have refused the dog), we allowed him to try. A week passed before the client returned with a photo: a laughing elderly man with a prosthetic leg in a golf cart with the terrier dog riding shotgun. The client explained to us that his neighbor was very despondent after his wife had died and would rarely leave the house. He was usually seen about the neighborhood in his golf cart, having lost a leg to complications of diabetes. They had a dog when the wife was alive but it had passed away, too. The elderly gentleman had become reclusive and people were worried about him. The terrier dog was the perfect medicine! The elderly man is now more active, engaging with his neighbors, and back to his golf cart outings with his new three-legged friend.

Loving companionship is not hard to find. It exists in wagging tails and warm puppy kisses. Dog ownership provides a need and a desire to carry on. It is a safe medicine for loneliness, depression, and anxiety. It may be just what the doctor ordered at some time in our lives. Never underestimate the power of high-quality, completely dedicated moral support that only a dog can provide. Their intuition is uncanny, and their devotion unmatched.

I once treated a lovely pit bull terrier that had been stabbed multiple times when she physically placed herself between her owner and the owner's abusive spouse. The woman was trampled down emotionally and feared leaving her husband, but seeing her loving and brave dog suffer at his hands propelled her to file charges, get a restraining order, and turn her life around. Her dog was the catalyst for her to seek help and leave her abuser. Those that have never spent a day in her shoes have no idea how hard this can be: the fear is all-consuming and destroys any thought of relief. Leaving the abuser means looking over your shoulder for months or years. A piece of paper won't keep him from stalking you, showing up at your home or work, and threatening you by his very presence. I felt her pain while helping the courageous little pit bull terrier, who had been stabbed multiple times. "Your dog is wonderful" is something she already knows. There are no words, only love.

Dogs often save us from our lives, our mistakes, our emotions, and ourselves. I have met so many heroes. They exist. They are real. They are in every neighborhood and half of American homes.

Your child will grow up and, hopefully, move out on his own. Don't let him transition alone. Make sure your child has a dog to help

navigate the social anomalies of life, all the maladies of adulthood, and living on his own. You and your child might not recognize it, but a dog can circumvent so many negative scenarios: loneliness, depression, introversion, and fear.

They simply have to be there for each other: a presence and a friend. The dog will hopefully not have to lay down its life for its family, but don't doubt that it would, given the necessary circumstance. When someone tells me their dog is the best dog in the world, I believe them. I know it to be true. I have heard many stories and met many heroes and I know their dog would do the extraordinary for them. They are the extraordinary. Be exceptional, and share it with a dog. He will understand. You can be fabulous together.

Chapter 8

Pet Death:
The Inevitable

Unfortunately, dogs live only about ten to fifteen years. During your child's progression to adulthood, he or she may have two to three dog companions, if not more. The hard consequence of having an animal that lives only about a decade is periodic heartache. This book is basically about the benefits that overwhelmingly outnumber the occasional sadness, so there is no need to reiterate the importance of getting another dog. Another dog will help with distraction and continued companionship. Remember, it is not about filling the holes; it's about giving a place for your love to go. Autism needs an outlet for emotions, and a new pet can help. Sadness will remain, there is no getting around it, but the saddest thing you can do is waste all the love and compassion you have by not getting another dog to share those feelings with.

Dogs do not fear death. We do. We fear the unknown. We cannot explain death except that it is the end of our time on this Earth, but it's not the end of our legacies. Someone may have memories of us that will live on. Your dog will have a legacy. His body will be gone, but the emotion attached to his history will remain. That's where the heartache can be transitioned to fondness and gratitude. Be thankful you shared his life. You were part of something great. Remember the high points and the good times. Be there for him at the end, if you can.

As your dog gets older, you may recognize that the inevitable is coming. Plan for it. Talk about it, if you can. Your dog cannot be there forever; nothing is forever. If possible, get another dog. The older dog can train the new one in the rules of your home. It can help the transition. It's not a replacement. It's just another companion, just another friend to guide us on the journey of life.

Many cultures believe the dog is the guide into the afterlife: Aztec, Greek, Mayan, and Tarascan. How better to be eased into the unknown than with your best friend at your side? Dogs guard the gates of the afterlife in many religions. They are there for us in our most trying times. The very diverse ancient cultures of Indians and Greeks have depicted the faithfulness of the dog written in The *Mahabharata* and the *Odyssey*: a loyal, devoted figure to his master, whether the master returns the devotion or not. You don't have to be good with dogs to be loved by dogs. A person with autism may not be good at expressing affection in the accepted human social way, but a dog will take whatever friendship is offered and return it in magnitude. He can build independence by fostering acceptance through consistent allegiance, which is a devotion recognized for centuries.

Man's survival on the planet has quite possibly been dependent on our relationship with the dog. Even the powerful, mythical beings of lore cherished their canine companions. The ancient Mesopotamian goddess Ishtar had seven hunting dogs. Many deities took the shape of the dog or used the dog to guard their possessions.

Dogs were used for protection and survival in primitive times. They gave man power to prevail in the toughest of times to continue their heritage by being whatever weapon or instrument man cared to wield.

Dogs are accepting of death. They don't know if they have an extra week or year on this planet by surviving an accident or cancer. They don't know if their condition is terminal or untreatable. They are there for you, right up to the end. So be there for them.

Should you have to make an appointment or show up at the emergency clinic to euthanize your dog, please stay with her. She trusts you. She knows you are sad and will be there to comfort you, as usual. This is one time you can be there for her as a small token for the years of service she has given. Don't take the collar off before she is gone if your dog normally wears it, it will distract her. You're upset, her collar is off—what's going on? She needs it to be just another veterinary visit.

Don't tell your children she is being "put to sleep," because it isn't true. As a child, I refused to sleep for weeks after my dog was "put to sleep," because I thought I would not return. I would collapse from exhaustion before laying down to sleep.

When your dog is being euthanized, her service is over. Euthanasia means "good death." This will probably be your child's first brush with death; sparing them this time may not help them in the long run because eventually, we all die. Try your best to explain this to them and describe the process. There are books available for managing pet loss, written for both children and adults. There are even pet loss support groups available by phone or visit. Dying is part of living. Your child needs to understand that the pet is dead and not just gone. There is no searching needed, there is no possibility of return. Death is not negotiable.

You don't necessarily have to have your child present at the euthanasia; it depends on the rationality of your child. As an emergency veterinarian, I see children at euthanasia procedures that understand and grasp the magnitude of the situation, and others that are hysterical and distracting for the parent and pet. You know your child. Say your goodbyes however best suits your child. Your pet has left you in charge of protecting your child's emotions during this time. Don't let her down.

Honesty is always the best protocol. Just because your child is young or has autism doesn't mean he should be coddled from the truth.

The opposite is true! I never understood pretending or cartoons or extravagant stories. I always wanted the hard facts, things that didn't have a variable outcome or irrational explanation. The truth stands on its own. It hurts at times, but it is predictable. You will get the same truth from every person explaining it. Unlike made-up things, the truth has history and is rational. The more honest we can be, the better. If your child gets the truth about your dog's illness and death, it will be easier to discuss later. Your child may have a memory like mine and will discuss a pet they had at four years of age like it was last week when it was actually forty years ago. Be prepared to remember all those little white lies you told, if that's the case, or you can make it easier on both of you if you just stick to the truth.

The euthanasia procedure is brief and painless. The dog is given an overdose of a sedative and falls asleep, then dies. Its last moments are focused on you, if you can bear to be present. If you are not present, the veterinary staff are always gentle and reverent. At my emergency clinic, we often offer him a last meal of lunch meat or tasty canned food and tell him what a good dog he has been. If he is experiencing pain, we give him pain medications first. When a pet dies, I have empathy, not sympathy. I have experienced the owner's pain in hearing about their dog's terminal illness or untimely death. Empathy is non-judgmental. Unlike sympathy, it is never condescending. I am sad in the moment, and I understand their pain. It is the one and only time I feel that I connect with strangers. It is raw and a bit scary. I allow myself to be vulnerable, to live in the moment and grieve.

I have loved and lost a pet. Sometimes I cannot fix pets when they are broken, including my own; sometimes I can.

Your child's sorrow may fester and manifest itself later. Be prepared to address it many times. Grief is a process, and the journey is long for many. If your child has autism, know that she carries a great deal of emotion with memories and sensory experiences, which can trigger her. There are certain warm and soft materials that induce my anguish of losing a dog because he habitually nested in a particular type of fabric bedding. I don't keep that type of fabric in my home because it makes me sad, just as sad as the day he died. The manifestation of his death and my pain are never dulled by the passing of time or number of exposures. Occasionally, the fabric shows up at the emergency clinic, when a pet is wrapped in it or a blanket is donated for our use. My pet dies all over again, and I am sad. I have autism, and it is a part of who I am for the rest of my life. Should your child with autism act seemingly irrational after the passing of her pet, try to find the trigger. It could be the dog's toy, bed, leash, or something special between them. You don't necessarily have to extinguish the response; you just need to be empathetic to the sequence.

Each of us manages our grief in our own way. I am quiet. I don't talk. I need to be alone, really alone, like out in the woods riding my horse or walking with my dog (I have more than one at all times). I don't want conversation, condolences, or hugs. I prefer to swing or rest in my hammock. It may take days before I am willing to engage again. Pet loss may be experienced by all of us, but we manage it individually. I have learned valuable lessons in coping, but I don't have the answers. I have a few tools and, now, a lot of experience. The pain is survivable. It hurts deeply because we care deeply. I may be an expert in the human-animal bond, but I am not immune to its powers. I give in easily to the friendly face of a new dog and the joys of the human/pet relationship. I know how it ends; I know that I will probably outlive many more dogs, but I have to conclude that the moments of sadness are worth a lifetime of love and memories.

After your pet has died, do something to honor his life. It may help you to heal. Plant a tree at his favorite spot in the yard. Put his ashes there if you can. Donate to the local shelter in his name. Do something that your child can interact with, so she can pay her respects to the dog.

The grieving process is important for healing. Acknowledge it. Go through the steps: denial, anger, bargaining, depression, and acceptance. You could also include shock, pain, guilt, reflection, loneliness, and then, hope. Have appropriate self-disclosure by telling your child how sad you are, too; how hard it is for you, also. Remember it isn't always sorrow. Share memories of joys and reminisce.

Veterinarian

Because I work in the emergency veterinary field, so many of our cases do not end well. Vets take a vow to use their scientific knowledge and skills for the benefit of society through the protection of animal welfare, the prevention and relief of animal suffering, and the promotion of public health. We understand that the human-animal bond is a mutually beneficial and dynamic relationship between people and animals, who are influenced by behaviors that are essential to the health and well-being of both. This includes, among other things, emotional, psychological, and physical interactions of people, animals, and the environment. The veterinarian's role in the human-animal bond is to maximize the potentials of this relationship between people and animals.

This degree of devotion and mental acuity comes at a cost to veterinarians. High levels of attachment, bond recognition, empathy, and love can lead to burn out, compassion fatigue, anxiety, and suicide. Veterinarians have one of the highest suicide rates in the nation because our patients only live about ten to fifteen years. Our careers often encompass the same family enduring heartache over and over again. Softening their pain by compassion can be exhausting.

Additionally, highly emotional clients are not always rational or kind. They can gravitate to anger very quickly. Fear can be the underlying motivator for their actions/emotions because their pet could be dying. Upset people don't have all the blood going to the rational sections of the brain. Instead, it shunts to the "flight or fight" response. It becomes pure emotion, which could be influenced by guilt about why the pet is in the condition he is, money issues, and/ or the fundamental fear of losing their pet. That emotion can then be projected toward the caregiver as we are trying to explain or provide alternatives, even escalating to accusations of malpractice, simply because the pet could not be saved.

The veterinary field is a caring profession. We spend years in

training and over a quarter million dollars in education to be there for your pet. We recognize your pain and attempt to mitigate it. But we also store all your pain, yesterday's pain, and any harsh words indefinitely, because we care. We are sad, too. We chose this profession to make a difference, and when the outcome is less than ideal, we all suffer.

Sometimes, we do save them. Sometimes we do make a difference. And sometimes, we get to observe the healing power of animals, regardless of our interventions. This must be why we keep getting dogs. We keep recognizing them as man's best friend and keep them in our homes, regardless of the heartache it sometimes brings. They have purpose. They are comforting. They have been there for us since the dawn of time, returning modicums of kindness with an avalanche of affection. Those are their best qualities: loyalty and love.

The dynamics of this affiliation are so weird. We don't speak each other's language, but we communicate. We teach a dog to hunt, to do police work, to find things. They tell us when there are drugs in searched vehicles, warn us of fires and impending danger, and occasionally save us from ourselves. They rescue us from danger and make uncompromised friendships with whomever chooses to love them back. You can truly be best friends from different species and never speak the same words.

Emergency veterinarians see death every day, sometimes up to ten or twenty times. Most veterinarians euthanize about six patients in a month, but emergency work is much different. We see only the worst cases. We make it as pleasant as possible. We love dogs, so this is hard for us, too. We understand it has to be done—all good things must come to an end. We can take away pain, we can save your dog her last bit of dignity and let her pass with peace and affection. We

are well-versed in the devastation that strong attachments and bonds induce at this time. Though normal, it is difficult, and no amount of verbiage will take away the ache.

Veterinarians that have examined the human-animal bond have determined that compassion fatigue is a real thing, which happens when veterinarians euthanize more than eight patients in a month. We, as veterinarians, understand how important animals are. Compassion fatigue was described for us as "the extreme state of tension and preoccupation with the suffering of those being helped to the degree that it can create a secondary traumatic stress for the helper (described by Dr. Charles Figley, a professor at Tulane Traumatology Institute in New Orleans)." Caring too much hurts. Just watching someone else hurt is painful. Pet death is horrible; no creature so pure and dedicated to human happiness should ever deserve to die, but she will. Be there for her so she is not left with strangers. Let her go quietly into the dark with your hand on her side and your voice in her ear.

If your veterinarian appears unaffected by your pet's passing, remember that being stoic may appear hard-hearted, and she may be just protecting her feelings. She may be trying to be strong for you or your child. She is attempting a balance of empathy and bravery. You have no idea what she is dealing with today or any other day. Maybe her own pet just died and she is trying to put on a brave face to just get through the day, so she can break down in tears at home. Your moment of duress may have been preceded by three others, and not everyone is kind when their pet's prognosis is grave. People lash out at their veterinarian, even if we are just the messenger. We can't save them all, and veterinary care has a cost. We are sorry to discuss financial constraints with clinical outcomes, but it is a fact of treatment. Sometimes it doesn't matter if you have all the money in the world; your pet isn't going to get better. Please don't take it out on the veterinarian. We are here to help. We care. We want to do what's best for your pet as much as you do, and sometimes euthanasia is the kindest choice. That's why it is a choice. We are supportive in your decision and will honor your reasoning, the decision to euthanize included.

I don't like that euthanasia is a part of my job, but I do my job. I usually cry. I am empathetic—I have been in your shoes. I know exactly what it is like to come home to an empty house and have no wagging tail to greet you at the door, have a dog bed with no dog, a toy with no pet to play with. I am sad in the moment and genuinely affected.

As soon as I leave the room, I find my toy poodle, Bazinga, to comfort me. Almost like a switch, I am sad but not pained to the point of crying. My empathy is real, but the pain is short. So, I can do it again. I can see the next patient. I can make the next diagnosis. I endure.

I hope you get another pet so you can have some relief, too.

You need another pet so you can continue with your life. The emptiness is real and devastating. Trust me when I tell you that I understand your pain. Another dog is not a replacement for your lost pet, but it's a diversion that may be the only relief possible.

Chapter 9

Dogs Understand Autism

I was told once that there is something "wrong" with me. The statement was very confusing. My dad has autism, thus I was raised by someone just like me. Is he "wrong," too? I was never told that I was any different than anybody else, and it was certainly never implied that something was "wrong" with me. There are many things "right" with me! I have an incredible memory and I have a genius IQ. I am very good at interacting with dogs. I have come to realize that the person who said this to me didn't understand autism. I'm not sure I understand autism. I think the only one who really understands me and my autism is my dog.

"Wrong" implies that someone needs to be fixed, which is simply incorrect. "Wrong" implies I'm not "normal." Should I be trained to be normal? Do I need or want to be normal? We are all different. I like being a unicorn in a world of normal! Negative opinions do not affect me because I was raised to embrace my difference. My family understood me, but the world does not.

Unfortunately, exposure to the social world can beat this confidence out of you. I was constantly corrected when I first went to college because I wasn't like everyone else. I was, at times, overwhelmed and frustrated. Having this experience as an adult instead of in childhood was probably easier to manage. I had established a high-quality coping mechanism with my dog. Since I didn't attend school until college, I wasn't bullied in elementary school and hadn't developed a callous attitude, which many people with autism do. Luckily, there is less bullying in college—but it does exist!

The majority of people in university settings are usually those with goals and dreams. They have outgrown the selfish tearing down of others and the perpetuating, exclusionary social groups. They have mostly grown up, because they are usually headed in a common direction towards a bachelor's degree or doctorate in a particular field.

They are social, which I am not. I do not yearn to be included, I simply yearn for acceptance. Just let me be. Let me exist without judgment or modification. I don't need companionship from them because I have my dogs. I just want kindness and to be treated with respect. Being different is okay.

My confidence in my differences was enhanced by my dad and by being sheltered from the grade and high school educational systems. I do not endorse homeschooling for your child and I don't promote the formal scholastic system, either. There are merits on both sides of the fence. Depending on where your child exists on the autism spectrum, one method of schooling might be more advantageous than the other and only you as a parent will know to what degree. The only thing I advocate for your child is to have empowerment by an overwhelming quantity of quality interactions. Small private schools may foster this and certain individuals within the typical school system can perpetuate it, but most importantly, your dog can instigate it.

The dog is wonderful therapy without a costly price tag. Your dog will understand your child, even if she is non-verbal, prone to outbursts, and/or a unicorn. Your dog will provide acceptance and companionship. He will understand any child, but particularly the child with autism.

Autism and its variables are "normal" to those of us on the spectrum and our dogs. On separate occasions, I have been told that I lack emotion or that I am overreacting and highly emotional. My husband, thankfully, accepts me anyway.

My sharply contrasting displays of response are rooted deep in sensory history. Though rational to me, "sensory" can be perplexing to others. When there is no history to pair to a particular setting, there is also no emotion. For example, if I were told that someone just wrecked their car, I have had no experience with that scenario and would have no reply; therefore, no emotion. My husband provides gentle guidance in what is deemed a "socially acceptable" reaction.

He knows I care about the person, but I don't care about cars. I didn't cause the wreck. I have no interaction or experience with the entire accident, but somehow I am expected to be surprised, sad, and empathetic. I take his guidance because he has vowed never to lead me astray. He keeps me appearing socially normal, though I don't understand it. He has never suggested that I was "wrong" or insisted that I change. He knows that I am different, and he is sure to let my dogs do their work when I am overwhelmed.

There are many people in your life and your child's life who can provide quality interactions and enhance development in a social setting. A dog can provide moral support during those times and an accepting, unconditional presence. Dogs know our moods better than we do. A dog could be the most influential therapy without a psychologist or prescription. He really understands autism in a way that is needed most. No other person may be able to rationalize the interaction, but trust that it works. It works for neurotypical people. It works for me.

Dogs "get" us and our habits. Recent studies have identified exactly how dogs read us so well. Their communication is only 10 percent

verbal. The rest is posture, carriage, gait, and facial expression. They can smell subtle hormones and sweat when we are afraid or nervous. No wonder they are perfect for a person with autism! We don't have to talk to them, they can just read us like a book. They recognize our introverted posturing and will attempt to coax us out of our shell. They engage us when we are sullen or afraid. They mitigate all manner of moods not associated with perpetual happiness. They speak our language.

Dogs learn by sensory and consistent, repetitive signals. They are very similar to people with autism in that they attach history to emotion. They can determine if a similar experience is going to be pleasant or uncomfortable based on previous situations. If there are no previous examples, they form a new opinion based on current events. Without a proper support system, the new experience can be frightening or induce anxiety. Leadership and an owner who has guided them through uncertain outcomes can teach the dog trust and give them a willingness to learn. The dog may step outside of its comfort zone and engage in new activities because previous events were successful. Their pattern of learning is similar to that of a person with autism, it's highly predictable when it is understood and completely irrational if you focus only on the sensory. A little bit of confidence blossoms into a mountain of hope, and a tiny bit of fear can be the initiation of an avalanche of reaction.

Dogs are also very good at pattern recognition. It baffles me that dogs are essentially color blind compared to humans but surpass us in pattern identification. They have greater visual acuity than humans and yet have no idea if their toy is red or green. They have seemingly eidetic (visual impressions that can be vividly and readily reproduced) memories, so they attach that memory to new things if it is even remotely similar. Their brains are reflective of those with autism and also neurotypicals, simultaneously being greater and deficient in certain aspects of both. I wish I could say I understand dogs because, at times, I think I communicate with them better than people, but I don't know why. I cannot explain our relationship; I just know that it is empowering and safely predictable. I don't know why they are so rewarding and painfully honest. I cannot explain their behavior or their cognitive function. Occasionally, I can modify a dog and train away certain aspects, but I cannot illuminate his pathway. Their exuberance at our very presence is baffling. Their love is undeserved. I have no words for their joy in life. Their presence is definitely needed.

They are like individuals on the autism spectrum: they assume that all is well and take everything at face value until circumstance dictates otherwise. They trust that everyone is kind and engaging and are, occasionally, oblivious to the insincerities of the general human population. They are okay with it. They forgive and forget, showing a child or person with autism that interactions are survivable and learnable. Most importantly, they are there when the person struggles. They are steadfastly loyal and merciful. They can help the emotionally unstable find comfort and reliability. You can be loud and upset, and they still love you. You can be sad and unreasonable and they are affectionate and devoted. Dogs defy reason.

I live on a farm wrapped in the woods of northern Idaho at the end of a dirt road. It is quiet and has ponds and horses and abundant wildlife. It is a safe zone from anxiety. It is a place of contentment for my autism, but it is not complete without my dog.

The solitude is welcome and peaceful; however, it is empty if my dog is not at my side. The old adage that a house is not a home without a dog is absolutely correct. If this can be true for a neurotypical person, imagine how much more it affects a person with autism, who is prone to anxiety as a portion of "normal" interactions and daily living. Even clutter can cause anxiety to a person with autism. These small prompts that can be most devastating and profound are often overlooked by the average person.

Our homes should be a safe zone, a place of peace and escape. If it is messy or busy or anything that influences the perception of harmony, anxiety becomes extreme. We have no reprieve. Our space is invaded, our home is destroyed. The gravity of the situation is ours to interpret. Remember, we are mostly sensory experience and emotion, so we are quick to accelerate to irrational. A dog can save us from ourselves. A dog makes our house a home.

My home is a place that does not require social interaction. Unlike my job, I can choose not to answer the phone. I don't have to have visitors. I can stay in the hammock all day or work in the garden. I am free. The social requirements of human interaction are not pursued unless I so desire that. And I adhere to no social constructs for interaction. I can work on a project with my husband or work alone. We can talk or we can just be quiet and together. Amazingly, this non-forced behavior makes me more willing to accept social behavior later on.

My home has dogs. It has a source of play and love and companionship that is unconditional. My home allows me a more active social life. It gives me confidence and nonjudgmental interactions. I feel empowered to converse with others because I have had a rewarding experience at home with my dogs. I can venture out and try new experiences, knowing I can always retreat to the sanctity of my home and the love of my dogs at any time. A few days at home to regroup and recharge, and I am ready to face the world again.

What an honor pet devotion is and how miraculously empowering. I feel that it is a privilege to be a part of the human-animal bond. Finding friends in this world is nearly impossible; there are few like-minded individuals to choose from, and the anomalies of autism are difficult for many to grasp. We don't offer a friendship that most people want to foster and it takes work to maintain our relationship. We rarely call, we don't initiate activities, and we are awkward at times. Sometimes we don't talk and sometimes we won't stop talking about a single subject. We are different. At times we appear to lack emotion and at others we are nothing but emotion. Not many people willingly choose to be our friend. Yet, we pick a dog, and he loves us. We decide we want the spotted one over the plain one, and we pick him, and he is 100 percent our dedicated friend. There is no introduction phase or getting-to-know-you phase. He just rejoices that he has a person and

that person is perfect in his eyes. The dog leaves his family, his home, and everything he has known up to this point in his life and he is happy about it! I don't know of any person capable of this kind of love. No wonder a dog makes a house a home. He brings joy and love with no measure. He is a miracle worker.

The households of people with autism have less anxiety when a dog lives there. Autism Speaks has done studies and states that parents and children are less stressed when a dog lives in the same home. The family is also more active and social. The dog gives the child a support system that cannot be mimicked with human interaction and, therefore, encourages more outgoing behavior.

The dog's presence can increase social skills and confidence. Gretchen Carlisle, who conducted the study on behalf of Autism Speaks' Treatment Networks states, "When I compared the social skills of children with autism who lived with dogs to those who did not, the children with dogs appeared to have greater social skills. More significantly, however, the data revealed that children with any kind of pet in the home reported being more likely to engage in behaviors such as introducing themselves, asking for information, or responding to other people's questions." A dog can initiate independence and assertiveness. It may be the one defining therapy to help in transitioning a child to adulthood and integration into society. A safe home can perpetuate safe outings. I would not have been able to negotiate the travails of my life and the complexities of my job if I had not had my dogs to see me through.

The obsessive-compulsive behavior typical of autism is actually very useful at home as well as in certain work settings. We clean and clean until it is just so. We put things away and make sure everything is well organized and neat. Retail facilities love this. We can stock shelves with all the labels pointed out and perfectly aligned. We fold our laundry to crisp corners and flat stacks. Our attention to detail and logical thinking can be assets. We take pride in our work and a job well done. We don't get wrapped up in inter-office drama or gossip. So, don't be afraid to disclose a condition of autism. It may actually be beneficial in securing a job.

With dogs, I rarely have sensory overload. I am not anxious when socially engaged. Their imminent presence isn't always the defining factor, they just have to be reasonably accessible. I can travel with my family on vacation and be less anxious knowing I can return to my dogs. My employees are very understanding and will video chat with me while they babysit our pets. I get to speak with my dog and see her activities, which gives me assurance she is happy and well cared for. I would like to believe that she misses me, but she makes the best of all her situations. She brings happiness to the world and she is happy to see me on my return. There is no greater reunion than human and dog! I love being recognized and cherished. I could be gone an hour

or a week, and the welcome is equally sincere and enthusiastic. It's wonderful to be loved and understood.

I hope that your home is blessed with the presence of a dog. Your appreciation of her services may not equal mine, and her support may be highly variable compared to mine, but I am sure she will bring joy and love. She may also enhance the social development of your child with autism. Whether her prowess can be measured or not, there is considerable evidence that it exists, which myriads of professionals can attest. She could strengthen your child's mental and physical health. A dog won't cure your child's autism, but she will love your child. A little love goes a long way. Some say it makes the world go 'round.

Dogs &Autism

Index: Dog Breeds and Information

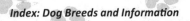

Index: Dog Breeds and Information

BREED	SIZE/WEIGHT (LBS)	ORIGINAL PURPOSE	COAT
Affenpinscher	Toy	Companion Dog	Scruffy
Afghan Hound	60	Sighthound and Pariah	Silky
Airedale Terrier	70	Terrier	Scruffy
Akbash	80	Guardian Dog	Fluffy
Akita	100	Northern Breed	Dense, Fluffy
Alaskan Husky	40	Northern Breed	Dense, Fluffy
Alaskan Klee Kai	Toy	Northern Breed	Dense, Fluffy
Alaskan Malamute	75	Utility	Dense, Fluffy
American Akita	100	Northern Breed	Dense, Fluffy
American Bulldog	50	Guardian Dog	Smooth
American Cocker Spaniel	25	Gun Dog	Silky
American English Coonhound	65	Scenthound	Smooth
American Eskimo Dog	Toy, 20, 35	Northern Breed	Dense, Fluffy
American Foxhound	65	Scenthound	Smooth

Dogs & Autism

BREED	SIZE/WEIGHT (LBS)	ORIGINAL PURPOSE	COAT
American Hairless Terrier	16	Terrier	None
American Pit Bull Terrier	55	Terrier	Smooth
American Staffordshire Terrier	55	Fighting	Smooth
American Water Spaniel	50	Gun Dog	Fluffy
Anatolian Shepherd Dog	Giant	Guardian Dog	Short, Dense, Fluffy
Anglo-Français de Petite Vénerie	50	Scenthound	Smooth
Appenzeller Sennenhund	50	Guardian Dog	Smooth
Ariegeois	50	Scenthound	Smooth
Australian Cattle Dog	50	Herding Dog	Short, Dense, Fluffy
Australian Kelpie	30	Herding Dog	Short
Australian Shepherd	40	Herding Dog	Fluffy
Australian Silky Terrier	Toy	Terrier	Silky

Index: Dog Breeds and Information

BREED	SIZE/WEIGHT (LBS)	ORIGINAL PURPOSE	COAT
Australian Stumpy Tail Cattle Dog	20	Herding Dog	Short
Australian Terrier	20	Terrier	Scruffy
Austrian Black and Tan Hound	50	Scenthound	Smooth
Austrian Pinscher	50	Terrier	Smooth
Azawakh	50	Sighthound and Pariah	Smooth
Barbet	50	Gun Dog	Fluffy
Basenji	22	Sighthound and Pariah	Smooth
Basset Hound	65	Scenthound	Smooth
Bavarian Mountain Hound	50	Scenthound	Short
Beagle	20, 30	Scenthound	Smooth
Bearded Collie	55	Herding Dog	Silky
Beauceron	110	Herding Dog	Smooth
Bedlington Terrier	20	Terrier	Scruffy
Belgian Shepherd Dog	60	Herding Dog	Fluffy

BREED	SIZE/WEIGHT (LBS)	ORIGINAL PURPOSE	COAT
Belgian Shepherd Dog (Malinois)	60	Herding Dog	Short, Dense, Fluffy
Bergamasco Shepherd	50	Herding Dog	Fluffy
Berger Blanc Suisse	50	Herding Dog	Fluffy
Berger Picard	70	Herding Dog	Fluffy
Bernese Mountain Dog	Giant	Guardian Dog	Fluffy
Bichon Frise	Toy	Companion Dog	Fluffy
Black and Tan Coonhound	110	Scenthound	Smooth
Black Mouth Cur	50	Scenthound	Smooth
Black Norwegian Elkhound	40	Northern Breed	Dense, Fluffy
Black Russian Terrier	130	Guardian Dog	Scruffy
Bloodhound	100	Scenthound	Smooth
Blue Heeler	40	Herding Dog	Short
Blue Picardy Spaniel	40	Gun Dog	Short
Bluetick Coonhound	100	Scenthound	Smooth
Boerboel	Giant	Guardian Dog	Smooth
Bolognese	Toy	Companion Dog	Fluffy

BREED	SIZE/WEIGHT (LBS)	ORIGINAL PURPOSE	COAT
Border Collie	55	Herding Dog	Dense, Fluffy
Border Terrier	Toy	Terrier	Scruffy
Borzoi	85	Sighthound and Pariah	Silky
Bosnian Coarse-haired Hound	50	Scenthound	Scruffy
Boston Terrier	25	Companion Dog	Smooth
Bouvier des Flandres	110	Herding Dog	Scruffy
Boxer	80	Guardian Dog	Smooth
Boykin Spaniel	50	Gun Dog	Short, Dense, Fluffy
Bracco Italiano	50	Gun Dog	Smooth
Briard	100	Herding Dog	Scruffy
Briquet Griffon Vendéen	60	Scenthound	Scruffy
Brittany	40	Gun Dog	Fluffy
Broholmer	Giant	Guardian Dog	Smooth
Bull Terrier	70	Terrier	Smooth
Bulldog	50	Companion Dog	Smooth
Bullmastiff	Giant	Guardian Dog	Smooth
Cairn Terrier	Toy	Terrier	Scruffy
Canaan Dog	45	Sighthound and Pariah	Short, Dense, Fluffy

BREED	SIZE/WEIGHT (LBS)	ORIGINAL PURPOSE	COAT
Canadian Eskimo Dog	40	Northern Breed	Dense, Fluffy
Cane Corso	Giant	Guardian Dog	Smooth
Carolina Dog	50	Sighthound and Pariah	Smooth
Catahoula Leopard Dog	50	Herding Dog	Smooth
Catalan Sheepdog	50	Herding Dog	Fluffy
Caucasian Shepherd Dog	Giant	Guardian Dog	Fluffy
Cavalier King Charles Spaniel	Toy	Companion Dog	Fluffy
Central Asian Shepherd Dog	40	Guardian Dog	Smooth
Cesky Terrier	20	Terrier	Scruffy
Chesapeake Bay Retriever	80	Gun Dog	Short
Chihuahua	Toy	Companion Dog	Smooth or Fluffy
Chinese Crested Dog	Toy	Companion Dog	Fluffy or None
Chow Chow	70	Northern Breed	Dense, Fluffy
Cirneco dell'Etna	25	Sighthound and Pariah	Smooth
Clumber Spaniel	75	Gun Dog	Fluffy
Collie, Rough	75	Herding Dog	Short

BREED	SIZE/WEIGHT (LBS)	ORIGINAL PURPOSE	COAT
Collie, Smooth	75	Herding Dog	Fluffy
Coton de Tulear	Toy	Companion Dog	Fluffy
Curly-Coated Retriever	80	Gun Dog	Short, Dense, Fluffy
Dachshund	20	Scenthound	Smooth or Short, Dense
Dalmatian	70	Companion Dog	Smooth
Dandie Dinmont Terrier	24	Terrier	Scruffy
Danish-Swedish Farmdog	50	Terrier	Smooth
Deutsche Bracke	50	Scenthound	Smooth
Doberman Pinscher	90	Guardian Dog	Smooth
Dogo Argentino	Giant	Guardian Dog	Smooth
Dogue de Bordeaux	Giant	Guardian Dog	Smooth
Dutch Shepherd	50	Herding Dog	Fluffy
English Cocker Spaniel	40	Gun Dog	Fluffy
English Foxhound	75	Scenthound	Smooth
English Setter	50	Gun Dog	Fluffy
English Shepherd	50	Herding Dog	Fluffy

BREED	SIZE/WEIGHT (LBS)	ORIGINAL PURPOSE	COAT
English Springer Spaniel	50	Gun Dog	Fluffy
English Toy Terrier (Black & Tan)	Toy	Companion Dog	Scruffy
Entlebucher Mountain Dog	80	Guardian Dog	Smooth
Estrela Mountain Dog	Giant	Guardian Dog	Fluffy
Eurasier	50	Northern Breed	Fluffy
Field Spaniel	50	Gun Dog	Fluffy
Fila Brasileiro	Giant	Guardian Dog	Smooth
Finnish Hound	50	Scenthound	Smooth
Finnish Lapphund	50	Northern Breed	Fluffy
Finnish Spitz	20	Northern Breed	Fluffy
Flat-Coated Retriever	50	Gun Dog	Fluffy
Fox Terrier, Smooth	20	Terrier	Smooth
Fox Terrier, Wire	20	Terrier	Scruffy
French Brittany	40	Gun Dog	Fluffy
French Bulldog	25	Companion Dog	Smooth
French Spaniel	40	Gun Dog	Fluffy

BREED	SIZE/WEIGHT (LBS)	ORIGINAL PURPOSE	COAT
Galgo Español	40	Sighthound and Pariah	Smooth
German Longhaired Pointer	50	Gun Dog	Scruffy
German Pinscher	50	Terrier	Smooth
German Roughhaired Pointer	50	Gun Dog	Scruffy
German Shepherd Dog	90	Herding Dog	Fluffy
German Shorthaired Pointer	50	Gun Dog	Smooth
German Spaniel	50	Gun Dog	Fluffy
German Spitz	20	Northern Breed	Dense, Fluffy
German Wirehaired Pointer	50	Gun Dog	Scruffy
Giant Schnauzer	Giant	Guardian Dog	Scruffy
Glen of Imaal Terrier	20	Terrier	Scruffy
Golden Retriever	60	Gun Dog	Fluffy
Gordon Setter	60	Gun Dog	Fluffy
Great Dane	Giant	Guardian Dog	Smooth
Great Pyrenees	Giant	Guardian Dog	Fluffy

BREED	SIZE/WEIGHT (LBS)	ORIGINAL PURPOSE	COAT
Greater Swiss Mountain Dog	Giant	Guardian Dog	Smooth
Greek Harehound	50	Scenthound	Smooth
Greenland Dog	80	Northern Breed	Short, Dense, Fluffy
Greyhound	70	Sighthound and Pariah	Smooth
Griffon Bruxellois	Toy	Companion Dog	Scruffy
Griffon Fauve de Bretagne	50	Scenthound	Scruffy
Hamiltonstövare	50	Scenthound	Smooth
Hanover Hound	80	Scenthound	Smooth
Harrier	60	Scenthound	Smooth
Havanese	Toy	Companion Dog	Silky
Hokkaido	60	Northern Breed	Short, Dense, Fluffy
Hovawart	80	Guardian Dog	Fluffy
Ibizan Hound	50	Sighthound and Pariah	Smooth
Icelandic Sheepdog	30	Herding Dog	Short, Dense, Fluffy
Irish Red and White Setter	50	Gun Dog	Fluffy
Irish Setter	50	Gun Dog	Fluffy

BREED	SIZE/WEIGHT (LBS)	ORIGINAL PURPOSE	COAT
Irish Terrier	30	Terrier	Scruffy
Irish Water Spaniel	50	Gun Dog	Fluffy
Irish Wolfhound	Giant	Sighthound and Pariah	Scruffy
Italian Greyhound	Toy	Companion Dog	Smooth
Jack Russell Terrier	20	Terrier	Smooth
Japanese Chin	Toy	Companion Dog	Silky
Japanese Spitz	20	Northern Breed	Fluffy
Japanese Terrier	20	Terrier	Smooth
Kangal Dog	Giant	Guardian Dog	Short, Dense, Fluffy
Karelian Bear Dog	60	Northern Breed	Short, Dense, Fluffy
Keeshond	40	Northern Breed	Fluffy
Kerry Blue Terrier	35	Terrier	Scruffy
King Charles Spaniel	30	Companion Dog	Silky
Kishu Ken	50	Northern Breed	Short, Dense, Fluffy
Komondor	Giant	Guardian Dog	Fluffy
Kooikerhondje	40	Gun Dog	Fluffy
Koolie	40	Herding Dog	Smooth

BREED	SIZE/WEIGHT (LBS)	ORIGINAL PURPOSE	COAT
Korean Jindo	50	Northern Breed	Short, Dense, Fluffy
Kromfohrländer	20	Companion Dog	Fluffy
Kuvasz	Giant	Guardian Dog	Fluffy
Labrador Retriever	80	Gun Dog	Smooth
Lagotto Romagnolo	50	Gun Dog	Fluffy
Lakeland Terrier	40	Terrier	Scruffy
Lancashire Heeler	30	Herding Dog	Sort, Dense, Fluffy
Leonberger	Giant	Guardian Dog	Fluffy
Lhasa Apso	20	Companion Dog	Silky
Löwchen	20	Companion Dog	Silky
Maltese	Toy	Companion Dog	Fluffy
Manchester Terrier	Toy, 20	Terrier	Smooth
Maremma Sheepdog	80	Guardian Dog	Fluffy
Mastiff	Giant	Guardian Dog	Smooth
McNab	40	Herding Dog	Smooth
Miniature American Shepherd	20	Herding Dog	Fluffy
Miniature Bull Terrier	20	Terrier	Smooth

BREED	SIZE/WEIGHT (LBS)	ORIGINAL PURPOSE	COAT
Miniature Pinscher	Toy	Companion Dog	Smooth
Miniature Schnauzer	20	Terrier	Scruffy
Münsterländer	50	Gun Dog	Fluffy
Neapolitan Mastiff	Giant	Guardian Dog	Smooth
Newfoundland	Giant	Guardian Dog	Fluffy
Norfolk Terrier	Toy	Terrier	Scruffy
Norrbottenspets	30	Northern Breed	Short, Dense, Fluffy
Norwegian Elkhound	55	Northern Breed	Fluffy
Norwich Terrier	Toy	Terrier	Scruffy
Nova Scotia Duck Tolling Retriever	50	Gun Dog	Fluffy
Old English Sheepdog	90	Herding Dog	Silky
Otterhound	110	Scenthound	Scruffy
Papillon	Toy	Companion Dog	Silky
Parson Russell Terrier	Toy	Terrier	Smooth
Pekingese	Toy	Companion Dog	Silky
Perro de Presa Canario	Giant	Guardian Dog	Smooth

BREED	SIZE/WEIGHT (LBS)	ORIGINAL PURPOSE	COAT
Peruvian Hairless Dog	40	Sighthound and Pariah	None
Petit Basset Griffon Vendéen	40	Scenthound	Scruffy
Pharaoh Hound	55	Sighthound and Pariah	Smooth
Plott Hound	60	Scenthound	Smooth
Podenco Canario	40	Sighthound and Pariah	Smooth
Pointer	70	Gun Dog	Smooth
Polish Greyhound	50	Sighthound and Pariah	Smooth
Polish Hound	50	Scenthound	Smooth
Polish Lowland Sheepdog	70	Herding Dog	Fluffy
Polish Tatra Sheepdog	Giant	Guardian Dog	Fluffy
Pomeranian	Toy	Companion Dog	Fluffy
Poodle	Toy, 20, 50	Companion Dog, Gun Dog	Fluffy
Portuguese Pointer	50	Gun Dog	Smooth
Portuguese Water Dog	60	Gun Dog	Fluffy
Pudelpointer	50	Gun Dog	Fluffy
Pug	Toy	Companion Dog	Smooth

BREED	SIZE/WEIGHT (LBS)	ORIGINAL PURPOSE	COAT
Puli	50	Herding Dog	Fluffy
Pumi	70	Herding Dog	Fluffy
Pyrenean Mastiff	Giant	Guardian Dog	Fluffy
Pyrenean Shepherd	30	Herding Dog	Fluffy
Rat Terrier	20	Terrier	Smooth
Redbone Coonhound	70	Scenthound	Smooth
Rhodesian Ridgeback	50	Sighthound and Pariah	Smooth
Romanian Mioritic Shepherd Dog	50	Herding Dog	Fluffy
Rottweiler	120	Guardian Dog	Smooth
Russell Terrier	Toy	Companion Dog	Smooth or Scruffy
Russian Spaniel	50	Gun Dog	Fluffy
Russian Toy	Toy	Companion Dog	Smooth
Russo-European Laika	50	Northern Breed	Short, Dense, Fluffy
Saarloos Wolfdog	50	Herding Dog	Short, Dense, Fluffy
Sabueso Español	50	Scenthound	Smooth
Saluki	65	Sighthound and Pariah	Silky

BREED	SIZE/WEIGHT (LBS)	ORIGINAL PURPOSE	COAT
Samoyed	65	Northern Breed	Fluffy
Schapendoes	50	Herding Dog	Fluffy
Schillerstövare	50	Scenthound	Smooth
Schipperke	Toy	Companion Dog	Dense, Fluffy
Scottish Deerhound	110	Sighthound and Pariah	Silky
Scottish Terrier	20	Terrier	Scruffy
Sealyham Terrier	25	Terrier	Scruffy
Segugio Italiano	20	Scenthound	Smooth
Serbian Hound	50	Scenthound	Smooth
Shar Pei	40	Northern Breed	Smooth
Shetland Sheepdog	25	Herding Dog	Fluffy
Shiba Inu	20	Northern Breed	Short, Dense, Fluffy
Shih Tzu	Toy	Companion Dog	Silky
Shikoku	50	Northern Breed	Short, Dense, Fluffy
Shiloh Shepherd	70	Herding Dog	Fluffy
Siberian Husky	60	Northern Breed	Dense, Fluffy
Silken Windhound	70	Sighthound and Pariah	Silky
Skye Terrier	40	Terrier	Silky

BREED	SIZE/WEIGHT (LBS)	ORIGINAL PURPOSE	COAT
Sloughi	50	Sighthound and Pariah	Smooth
Slovak Cuvac	Giant	Guardian Dog	Fluffy
Slovakian Wirehaired Pointer	50	Gun Dog	Scruffy
Slovenský Kopov	50	Scenthound	Smooth
Soft-Coated Wheaten Terrier	40	Terrier	Scruffy
Spanish Mastiff	Giant	Guardian Dog	Smooth
Spanish Water Dog	60	Herding Dog	Fluffy
Spinone Italiano	55	Gun Dog	Scruffy
Sporting Lucas Terrier	20	Terrier	Scruffy
St. Bernard	Giant	Guardian Dog	Fluffy
Staffordshire Bull Terrier	40	Terrier	Smooth
Standard Schnauzer	50	Guardian Dog	Scruffy
Sussex Spaniel	50	Gun Dog	Fluffy
Swedish Lapphund	50	Northern Breed	Fluffy
Swedish Vallhund	40	Herding Dog	Short, Dense, Fluffy
Teddy Roosevelt Terrier	20	Terrier	Smooth

BREED	SIZE/WEIGHT (LBS)	ORIGINAL PURPOSE	COAT
Tibetan Mastiff	Giant	Guardian Dog	Fluffy
Tibetan Spaniel	Toy	Companion Dog	Fluffy
Tibetan Terrier	30	Companion Dog	Fluffy
Tornjak	Giant	Guardian Dog	Fluffy
Tosa	70	Guardian Dog	Smooth
Toy Fox Terrier	Toy	Terrier	Smooth
Toy Manchester Terrier	Toy	Terrier	Smooth
Transylvanian Hound	50	Scenthound	Smooth
Treeing Cur	50	Scenthound	Smooth
Treeing Tennessee Brindle	50	Scenthound	Smooth
Treeing Walker Coonhound	50	Scenthound	Smooth
Tyrolean Hound	40	Scenthound	Smooth
Vizsla	60	Gun Dog	Smoth
Volpino Italiano	20	Northern Breed	Smooth
Weimaraner	90	Gun Dog	Smooth
Welsh Corgi, Cardigan	40	Herding Dog	Short, Dense, Fluffy
Welsh Corgi, Pembroke	40	Herding Dog	Short, Dense, Fluffy

BREED	SIZE/WEIGHT (LBS)	ORIGINAL PURPOSE	COAT
Welsh Sheepdog	40	Herding Dog	Short, Dense, Fluffy
Welsh Springer Spaniel	40	Gun Dog	Fluffy
Welsh Terrier	20	Terrier	Scruffy
West Highland White Terrier	20	Terrier	Scruffy
West Siberian Laika	50	Northern Breed	Fluffy
Westphalian Dachsbracke	40	Scenthound	Short, Dense, Fluffy
Wetterhoun	80	Gun Dog	Fluffy
Whippet	40	Sighthound and Pariah	Smooth
White Shepherd	70	Herding Dog	Fluffy
Wirehaired Pointing Griffon	70	Gun Dog	Scruffy
Wirehaired Vizsla	65	Gun Dog	Scruffy
Xiasi Dog	40	Gun Dog	Fluffy
Xoloitzcuintli	Toy, 30, 55	Sighthound and Pariah	None
Yorkshire Terrier	Toy	Companion Dog	Silky

Toy = less than 20 pounds
Giant = greater than 110 pounds
Terriers are rodent hunters, Northern breeds pull sleds

About the Author

Annie Bowes was diagnosed with autism as an adult, which didn't limit her ability to become an emergency and critical care veterinarian. Dr. Bowes' unique background was greatly influenced by her ASD father who encouraged her to focus on the gifts that autism can bring, not how she differed from the world.

Dr. Bowes is an authority on the human-animal bond, has completed the human-animal bond certification program at Purdue University, and consults for the Pet Loss Support Group and other human-animal bond programs designed to understand the connection between pets to their owners. The emergency veterinary field brings the most emotional and trying experiences, giving Dr. Bowes unparalleled exposure to the richness of the pet connection and the capacities of the human spirit. Her books reflect her time witnessing the miracle and privilege of the pet relationship.

DID YOU LIKE THE BOOK?

Rate it and share your opinion.

amazon.com   **BARNES&NOBLE**
BOOKSELLERS
www.bn.com

Not what you expected? Tell us!

Most negative reviews occur when the book did not reach expectation. Did the description build any expectations that were not met? Let us know how we can do better.

Please drop us a line at *info@fhautism.com*.
Thank you so much for your support!